Level 1 Part 1

Integrated Chinese
中文聽說讀寫

Traditional Character Edition
Character Workbook

Tao-Chung Yao, Yuehua Liu
Xiaojun Wang, Yea-fen Chen, Liangyan Ge
with Jeffrey J. Hayden

Cheng & Tsui Company

First edition 1997
2002 Printing

Cheng & Tsui Company
25 West Street
Boston, MA 02111-1213 USA

Traditional Character Edition
ISBN 0-88727-266-5

Companion textbooks, workbooks and audio tapes are also available from the publisher.

Printed in the United States of America

PUBLISHER'S NOTE

The Cheng & Tsui Company is pleased to announce the most recent addition to its Asian Language Series, *Integrated Chinese*. This entirely new course program for the beginning to advanced student of Mandarin Chinese will incorporate textbooks, workbooks, character workbooks, teaching aids, audio tapes, video tapes, CD-ROM computer programs and interactive multimedia programs. Field-tested since 1994, this series has been very well received. It is our intention to keep it a dynamic product by continuing to add, revise and refine the content as we get your valuable feedback.

This series seeks to train students in all four language skills: listening, speaking, reading and writing. It utilizes a variety of pedagogical approaches—grammar translation, audio-lingual, direct method, total physical response—to achieve the desired results. Because no two Chinese language programs are the same, *Integrated Chinese* provides those classes that cover the lessons more speedily with additional material in the form of Supplementary Vocabulary. The Supplementary Vocabulary section, however, is purely optional.

The *C&T Asian Language Series* is designed to publish and widely distribute quality language texts as they are completed by such leading institutions as the Beijing Language Institute, as well as other significant works in the field of Asian languages developed in the United States and elsewhere.

We welcome readers' comments and suggestions concerning the publications in this series. Please contact the following members of the Editorial Board:

Professor Shou-hsin Teng, Chief Editor
3 Coach Lane, Amherst, MA 01002

Professor Dana Scott Bourgerie
Asian and Near Eastern Languages, Brigham Young University, Provo, UT 84602

Professor Samuel Cheung
Dept. of Oriental Languages, University of California, Berkeley, CA 94720

Professor Ying-che Li
Dept. of East Asian Languages, University of Hawaii, Honolulu, HI 96822

Professor Timothy Light
Office of the Provost, Western Michigan University, Kalamazoo, MI 49008

Table of Contents

Preface

This *Character Workbook* is a companion volume to *Integrated Chinese, Textbook, Level I, Part 1 (Traditional Character Version)*. *Integrated Chinese* is a series of Chinese language textbooks written by the *Integrated Chinese* committee which consistes of seven members (Nyan-ping Bi, Yea-fen Chen, Liangyan Ge, Yuehua Liu, Yaohua Shi, Xiaojun Wang, and Tao-chung Yao). The first two levels of *Integrated Chinese* are available now. In addition to this *Character Workbook*, there is another workbook for students to learn the four language skills (listening, speaking, reading, and writing).

This book is designed to help the student to learn Chinese characters in their correct stroke order, and then by components. We believe that the student will learn a new character more easily if he/she can identify the components in each character and know why the specific components are used in each character. Therefore we strongly urge teachers to teach their students the 40 basic radicals which are frequently used to compose Chinese characters.

When learning a new character, the first thing that the student should do is to try to identify the known component(s). By doing that, the student will only need to remember what components are in the character, rather than remember the composition of many meaningless strokes. For example, both 女 (nǚ, female) and 馬 (mǎ, horse) are taught in the radical section. When the student sees the character 媽 (mā, mother) in Lesson 2, he/she should be able to tell that the new character 媽 consists of two known components, namely, 女 and 馬. The components in a character sometimes give clues to the meaning and pronunciation of the character. The radical 女 in the character 媽 suggests that the character might be related to females and the other component, 馬, is a phonetic element giving a clue to its pronunciation. If a student can remember that the character for "mother" sounds like "horse", he/she would have an easier time learning how to write the character. It would be a very painful way to learn the character 媽 if all one sees is a character consisting of a number of meaningless strokes, with a few vertical lines, a few horizontal lines, a few dots, etc.

The 40 radicals selected here, of course, are just some of the components that are seen in Chinese characters. However, by mastering these 40 radicals the student will realize that many characters contain one or two of the 40 components, and that the student only need to concentrate on the new components which he/she has not seen before. By knowing the meanings and the pronunciations of the components of the new character, the student will be able to retain the shape and the sound of the new character better.

After the radicals section in this workbook there is a small section for numerals. Since numerals are extremely useful in everyday life, we urge students to learn the characters 1-10 as soon as possible. Also, these characters are quite easy to write and can serve as a good introductory lesson for beginning students.

Each page of this *Character Workbook* has three to four new characters on it. Each new character is displayed in a large point size on the left side of the page, with its *pinyin* reading and English translation immediately to the right. Next to the *pinyin* reading there is a number in parentheses. The number indicates the ranking of the character given in the <u>Xiàndài Hànyǔ Pínlù Cídiǎn</u> (《現代漢語頻率詞典 》, *The Dictionary of Modern Chinese Word Frequency*). For example, for the character 人 (rén, person), the number "9" given in the parentheses means that this character is the ninth most frequently used character in the Chinese language.

The symbol "†" in the parentheses indicates that the character does not belong to the 1000 most frequently used characters according to the <u>Xiàndài Hànyǔ Pínlù Dà Cídiǎn</u>. While we try to introduce the first 1000 most frequently used characters in the first two levels of *Integrated Chinese*, we sometimes have to include some characters beyond the first thousand to make the text natural and functional.

In the radical section, under the English translation of the radical, a smaller size of the same character is found. If the radical has a variation, then the variation is given to the right side of the smaller character. In the main lessons, the simplified version of the character is given to the right of the smaller traditional character. Occasionally the character to the right will have the small symbol "Δ" after it indicating the printing form. Students should learn how to write the written form, i.e., the character to the left of it. Each practicing unit for a character contains three or four rows of small boxes. The first row has a grayed version of the character. The student is expected to trace this. The second row is in graph-style layout to facilitate practice at character proportion. The third row and the remaining empty boxes are for the student to practice writing the character. By this time, the student can be expected to be able to draw the character in proper spatial proportions without the use of any guides.

The textbook for *Integrated Chinese* was done using TwinBridge on an IBM-PC computer and this *Character Workbook* was done on a Macintosh. There were some problems finding the right character in the computer. For example, the traditional character for niàn (to read) should be 唸, but it does not exist in TwinBridge, so the textbook uses the simplified form 念. However, students should learn how to write the traditional form as shown in this *Character Workbook*. There are two ways to write the traditional character for lǐ (inside), 裏 and 裡. However, the Macintosh only has

裡. That is why this *Character Workbook* teaches students how to write 裡 rather than the 裏 used in the textbook. Other examples inlude 床／牀, 黃／黄, etc. We hope we can solve this technical problem in the next edition.

It is very important that each character is drawn in the correct stroke order. Two devices are used in this workbook to show a character's stroke order. The small numbers printed along the large characters indicate the sequence of the strokes. In general, every effort has been made to place the number at the starting point of the stroke. Because in some instances it is not very easy to tell which number goes with what stroke, or to tell where each stroke begins and ends, a "pen version" of each character is provided. Right below the large character, the character is drawn one step at a time to show how it is formed. Students should consult with this series of strokes when practicing writing characters.

For components which have previously appeared, the pen version may simply show the entire component already drawn rather than writing it out one stroke at a time. For example, the pen version for the character 明 (míng, bright) in Lesson 4 only uses two boxes, one for 日, and one for 明. This means that when writing the character 明, one first writes 日, and then one writes 月 next to 日 to form 明. No individual strokes are given here because the student has already learned how to write 日, and 月 separately.

There are many computer programs (such as *Chinese Character Tutor* by Ted Yao and Mark Peterson and *Hanzi Assistant* by Panda Software) which are designed to teach stroke order. Students are encouraged to use them if they have access to the software. For more information on computer software for learning Chinese characters, please see our home page at <http://www.lll.hawaii.edu/ICUsers/>.

The three people who have spent the most time in preparing this *Character Workbook* are Tao-chung Yao, Jeffrey J. Hayden, and Xiaojun Wang. Yao designed the format for the first two versions (1994, 1995) and wrote the stroke numbers by hand. Wang did the calligraphy for the very first version (1994) and has also done most of the the pen version stroke ordering in this current edition. Yao and Hayden collaborated on the 1996 and 1997 editions. Yao has been responsible for the overall planning, and Hayden has translated Yao's ideas into the current form, including entering all of the data and numbering each stroke. We would like to thank Mr. Song Jiang for doing the pen version stroke ordering for Lessons 2 through 11 for this volume on such short notice.

人	rén (9) man; person	人	亻	人	人	人	人	人	人
丿	人 亻								
丿	人 亻								

刀	dāo (789) knife	刀	刂	刀	刀	刀	刀	刀	刀
フ	刀 刂								
フ 丶	刀 刂								

力	lì (119) power	力		力	力	力	力	力	力
フ 力									

又	yòu (65) right hand; again	又		又	又	又	又	又	
フ 又									

口	kǒu (182) mouth	口	口	口	口	口	口
	口						
丶	冂	口					

口	**wéi (†) enclose	口	口	口	口	口	口
	口						
丨	冂	口					

** Used as a radical only, not as a character by itself.

土	tǔ (373) earth	土	土	土	土	土	土
	土						
一	十	土					

夕	xī (†) sunset	夕	夕	夕	夕	夕	夕
	夕						
丿	勹	夕					

大	dà (17) big; large	大	大	大	大	大	大
	大						
一	ナ	大					

女	nǚ (299) female; woman	女	女	女	女	女	女
	女						
𡿨	女	女					

子	zǐ (24) son	子	子	子	子	子	子
	子						
乛	了	子					

寸	cùn (寸) inch	寸	寸	寸	寸	寸	寸
	寸						
一	寸	寸					

小	xiǎo (50) little; small	小	小	小	小	小	小
	小						
㇓	小	小					

工	gōng (55) labor; work	工	工	工	工	工	工
	工						
一	丁	工					

幺	yāo (†) tiny; small	幺	幺	幺	幺	幺	幺
	幺						
ㄥ	幺	幺					

弓	gōng (†) bow	弓	弓	弓	弓	弓	弓
	弓						
ㄱ	コ	弓					

心	xīn (82) heart	心	心	心	心	心	心
	心 忄						
丶 八 心 心							
丶 八 忄							

戈	gē (忄) dagger-axe	戈	戈	戈	戈	戈	戈
	戈						
一 弋 戈 戈							

手	shǒu (115) hand	手	手	手	手	手	手
	手 扌						
一 二 三 手							
一 十 扌							

日	rì (269) sun	日	日	日	日	日	日
	日						
丨 冂 日 日							

		yuè (207) moon	月	月	月	月	月	月
月		月						
丿	刀	月	月					

		mù (607) wood	木	木	木	木	木	木
木		木						
一	十	才	木					

		shuǐ (102) water	水	水	水	水	水	水
水		水	氵					
亅	刁	水	水					
丶	冫	氵						

		huǒ (308) fire	火	火	火	火	火	火
火		火	灬					
丶	⼩	少	火					
丿	八	灬	灬					

田	tián (727) field	田	田	田	田	田	田
	田						
丨	冂	冃	用	田			

目	mù (408) eye	目	目	目	目	目	目
	目						
丨	冂	月	月	目			

示	shì (†) to show	示	示	示	示	示	示
	示	礻					
一	二	于	亓	示			
丶	㇇	礻	礻				

糸	**mì (†) fine silk	糸	糸	糸	糸	糸	糸
	糸	幺					
厶	幺	幺	糸	糸	糸		
厶	幺	幺	幺	糸	糸		

** Used as a radical only, not as a character by itself.

耳	ěr (960) ear	耳	耳	耳	耳	耳	耳
	耳						
一	丁	干	开	耳	耳		

衣	yī (473) clothing	衣	衣	衣	衣	衣	衣
	衣	衤					
、	二	亠	犬	衣	衣		
、	冫	衤	衤	衤			

言	yán (655) speech	言	言	言	言	言	言
	言						
、	亠	亠	言	言	言	言	

貝	bèi (†) cowry shell	貝	貝	貝	貝	貝	貝
	貝						
丨	冂	月	月	目	貝	貝	

走	zǒu (104) to walk	走	走	走	走	走	走
	走						
一	十	土	キ	キ	走	走	

足	zú (758) foot	足	足	足	足	足	足
	足	𧾷					
丶	口	口	𩙿	𨈐	足	足	
丶	口	口	𩙿	𨈐	足	足	

金	jīn (514) metal; gold	金	金	金	金	金	金
	金						
丿	人	亼	今	全	余	仐	金

門	mén (199) door	門	門	門	門	門	門
	門						
丨	𠃌	門	門	門	門	門	門

隹	zhuī (†) short-tailed bird	隹	隹	隹	隹	隹
	隹					
ノ	亻	个	仁	仁	仨	隹

雨	yǔ (542) rain	雨	雨	雨	雨	雨	雨
	雨	雲					
一	冖	冂	币	雨	雨	雨	
一	冖	二	平	雫	雫	雫	雫

食	shí (549) to eat	食	食	食	食	食	食
	食	食					
ノ	人	仝	今	今	含	食	食	食
ノ	亽	夂	今	今	含	食	食	

馬	mǎ (359) horse	馬	馬	馬	馬	馬	馬
	馬						
一	厂	戸	戶	馬	馬	馬	馬	馬

	yī (2) one							
一	一							
一								

	èr (118) two							
二	二							
一	二							

	sān (106) three							
三	三							
一	二	三						

	sì (166) four							
四	四							
丨	冂	兀	四	四				

五	wǔ (195) five	五	五	五	五	五	五
	五						
一 丁 万 五							

六	liù (358) six	六	六	六	六	六	六
	六						
丶 亠 宀 六							

七	qī (393) seven	七	七	七	七	七	七
	七						
一 七							

八	bā (323) eight	八	八	八	八	八	八
	八						
丿 八							

九	jiǔ (264) nine	九	九	九	九	九	九
	九						
ノ 九							

十	shí (79) ten	十	十	十	十	十	十
	十						
一 十							

Dialogue I

先	xiān (179) first	先	先	先	先	先	先
	先						
ノ 𠂉 牛 生 先 先							

生	shēng (42) to be born	生	生	生	生	生	生
	生						
ノ 𠂉 仁 牛 生							

你	nǐ (20) you	你	你	你	你	你	你
	你						
亻 亻 你 你							

好	hǎo (40) fine; good; OK	好	好	好	好	好	
	好						
女 好							

小	xiǎo (50) little; small	小	小	小	小	小	小
	小						
小							

姐	jiě (693) older sister	姐	姐	姐	姐	姐	姐
	姐						
女	女	如	如	姐	姐		

王	wáng (863) (a surname); king	王	王	王	王	王	
	王						
一	二	干	王				

李	lǐ (†) (a surname); plum	李	李	李	李	李	
	李						
木	李						

Dialogue II

請	qǐng (547) please; to invite	請	請	請	請	請
	請　请					
言　言　言　訁　訡　請						

問	wèn (112) to ask	問	問	問	問	問	問
	問　问						
門　問							

您	nín (237) you (polite)	您	您	您	您	您	您
	您						
你　您							

貴	guì (†) honorable; expensive	貴	貴	貴	貴	貴
	貴　贵					
丶　冂　口　中　虫　貴						

姓	xìng (†) surname	姓	姓	姓	姓	姓	姓
	姓						
女 姓							

我	wǒ (6) I; me	我	我	我	我	我	我
	我						
ノ 二 千 手 扰 我 我							

呢	ne (151) QP	呢	呢	呢	呢	呢	呢
	呢						
口 口ヿ 口コ 吓 呎 呢							

叫	jiào (154) to be called	叫	叫	叫	叫	叫	叫
	叫						
口 口L 叫							

什	shén (80) *what	什	什	什	什	什	什
	什 甚						
亻 什							

(Note: The simplified form is taught here because the traditional form is rarely used now.)

麼	me (27) *QP	麼	麼	麼	麼	麼	麼
	麼 么						
丶	广	广	广	斤	庐	床	床	麻	麻
麻 麼							

名	míng (410) name	名	名	名	名	名	名
	名						
夕 名							

字	zì (409) character	字	字	字	字	字	字
	字						
丶	宀	宀	字				

	péng (628) friend	朋	朋	朋	朋	朋	朋
朋	朋						
月 朋							

	yǒu (485) friend	友	友	友	友	友	友
友	友						
一 ナ 友							

Dialogue III

是	shì (4) to be	是	是	是	是	是	是
	是						
日	旦	是	旱	异	是		

老	lǎo (87) old	老	老	老	老	老	老
	老						
一	十	土	耂	老	老		

師	shī (310) teacher	師 师	師	師	師	師	師
丿	亻	阝	阝	㠯	㠯	㠯	帥	師	師

嗎	ma (248) QP	嗎	嗎	嗎	嗎	嗎	嗎
	嗎 吗						
口	嗎						

不	bù (5) not; no	不	不	不	不	不	不
	不						
一	丆	不	不				

學	xué (46) to study	學	學	學	學	學	學
	學	学					
丶	亻	乍	乍	乍	乍	乍	臼	臼	臼
臼	臼	臼	臼	學	學	學			

也	yě (30) too; also	也	也	也	也	也	也
	也						
刁	九	也					

中	zhōng (61) center; middle	中	中	中	中	中	
	中						
丨	冂	口	中				

國	guó (37) country	國	國	國	國	國	國
	國 国						
一	冂	冂	同	同	国	国	國	國	

人	rén (9) person; people	人	人	人	人	人
	人					
丿	人					

美	měi (593) beautiful	美	美	美	美	美	美
	美						
丶	丷	兰	兰	羊	羊	美		

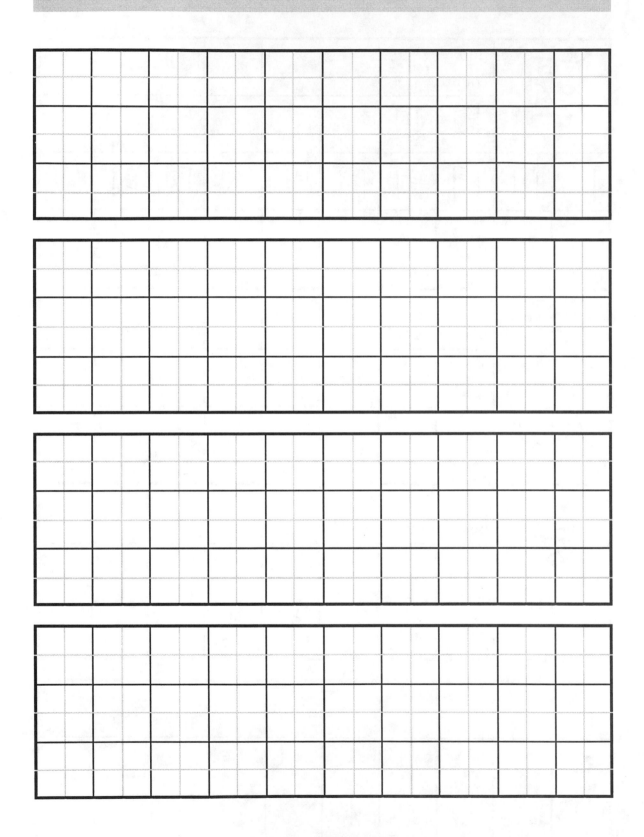

Dialogue I

那	nà / nèi (31) that	那	那	那	那	那	那
	那						
ㄱ	ㄱ	ㄱ	尹	尹ノ	尹了	那	

張	zhāng (431) M; (a surname)	張	張	張	張	張	
	張 张						
弓	弓	引	引	引	張	張	張	張

照	zhào (388) to shine	照	照	照	照	照	照
	照						
日	日	昭	照				

片	piàn (413) *film; slice	片	片	片	片	片	片
	片						
ノ	冫	丬	片				

的	de P (1)	的	的	的	的	的	的
	的						
ノ	白	白	的	的			

這	zhè / zhèi (10) this	這	這	這	這	這	這
	這 这						
言	言	言	言	這			

爸	bà (390) dad	爸	爸	爸	爸	爸	爸
	爸						
ノ	八	父	父	父	谷	谷	爸

媽	mā (180) mom	媽	媽	媽	媽	媽	媽
	媽 妈						
女	媽						

個	gè (14) M (general)	個	個	個	個	個	個
	個 个						
亻 亻 们 佣 佃 個 個							

男	nán (937) male	男	男	男	男	男	男
	男						
田 男							

孩	hái (304) child	孩	孩	孩	孩	孩	孩
	孩						
子 孑 孑 孑 孩 孩 孩							

子	zǐ (24) son; child	子	子	子	子	子	子
	子						
乛 了 子							

誰	shéi (353) QW; who?	誰	誰	誰	誰	誰	誰
	誰 谁						
言 誰							

他	tā (11) he; him	他	他	他	他	他	他
	他						
亻 他							

弟	dì (431) younger brother	弟	弟	弟	弟	弟	
	弟						
丶 丷	㇉ 弔 弖 弟 弟						

女	nǔ (299) female; woman	女	女	女	女	女	
	女						
女							

	mèi (912)		妹	妹	妹	妹	妹
妹	younger sister						
	妹						
女	女	妡	奸	姝	妹		

	tā (74)		她	她	她	她	她	她
她	she							
	她							
女	她							

	ér (378)		兒	兒	兒	兒	兒	兒
兒	son; child							
	兒	儿						
ﾉ	𠂉	𠂉	臼	臼	臼	臼	兒	

	yǒu (8)		有	有	有	有	有	有
有	to have							
	有							
一	ナ	有						

没	méi (51) (to have) not	没	没	没	没	没	没
	没 没△						
シ	シ	沙	没				

高	gāo (105) (a surname); tall	高	高	高	高	高	
	高						
丶	亠	古	宁	高	高		

Dialogue II

家	jiā (56) family; home	家	家	家	家	家	家
	家						
丶	丷	宀	宀	宁	宁	宇	家	家	家

幾	jǐ (124) how many?	幾	幾	幾	幾	幾	幾
	幾	几					
幺	丝	丝	丝	丝	幾	幾	幾	

哥	gē (489) older brother	哥	哥	哥	哥	哥	哥
	哥						
一	口	可	哥	哥	哥			

兩	liǎng (103) two; a couple of	兩	兩	兩	兩	兩	
	兩	两					
一	厂	门	兩	兩	兩	兩	兩	

和	hé (23) and 和	和	和	和	和	和	和
ノ	禾	和					

做	zuò (168) to do; to make 做	做	做	做	做	做	
亻	什	估	估	做	做	做	

英	yīng (915) *England 英	英	英	英	英	英	英
ノ	十	艹	艹	艹	苎	苎	苹	英

文	wén (170) (written) language; script 文	文	文	文	文
、	一	亠	文		

律	lǜ (683) law; rule	律	律	律	律	律	律
	律						
ノ	ノ	彳	彳	行	行	律	律

都	dōu (48) all; both	都	都	都	都	都	都
	都						
一	十	土	少	者	者	者	都

醫 see page 135	yī (646) doctor; medicine	醫	醫	醫	醫	醫	
	醫 医						
一	厂	匚	匸	歹	医	医	医
殴	殴	醫	醫	醫	醫	醫	醫

Dialogue I

月	yuè (207) month; moon	月	月	月	月	月
	月					
月						

號	hào (559) number	號	號	號	號	號	號
	號	号					
口	口	号	号	号	号	号	号	號
號							

星	xīng (499) star	星	星	星	星	星	星
	星						
日	星						

期	qī (342) period (of time)	期	期	期	期	期
	期					
一	十	廿	甘	甘	其	其	其	期

天	tiān (54) sky; heaven; day	天	天	天	天	天
	天					
一	天					

日	rì (269) sun; day	日	日	日	日	日
	日					
日						

今	jīn (297) today; now	今	今	今	今	今
	今					
人	亽	今				

年	nián (49) year	年	年	年	年	年
	年					
丿	一	仁	午	上	年	

多	duō (53) many	多	多	多	多	多	多	多
	多							
夕	多							

大	dà (17) big	大	大	大	大	大	大
	大						
大							

歲	suì (617) age	歲	歲	歲	歲	歲	歲
	歲 岁						
丨	卜	屮	止	芦	芦	芦	芦	芦
歲	歲	歲					

吃	chī (217) to eat	吃	吃	吃	吃	吃	吃
	吃						
口	口′	叱	吃				

晚	wǎn (455) evening; late	晚	晚	晚	晚	晚	晚
	晚						
日	日	日	日	昉	晘	晘	晚	晚

(Please note that strokes 9 and 11 are two separate strokes.)

飯	fàn (552) meal	飯	飯	飯	飯	飯	飯
	飯	饭					
食	食	飣	飯				

怎	zěn (173) *how	怎	怎	怎	怎	怎	怎
	怎						
ノ	ト	乍	乍	乍	怎		

樣	yàng (70) form; kind	樣	樣	樣	樣	樣	樣
	樣	样					
木	样	样	样	样	樣	樣	

太	tài (214) too; extremely	太	太	太	太	太
	太					
大 太						

了	le (3) P	了	了	了	了	了	了
	了						
㇖ 了							

謝	xiè (861) to thank	謝	謝	謝	謝	謝	謝
	謝 谢						
言	言	訂	訇	訶	詶	訽	謝

喜	xǐ (608) to like; happy	喜	喜	喜	喜	喜	喜
	喜						
一	十	士	吉	吉	言	壴	喜

| 歡 huān (592) joyful see page 135 | 歡 欢 | 歡 歡 歡 歡 歡 | |
| 卄 甘 茁 藿 藿 藿 歡 | | | |

還 hái (45) still; yet	還 还	還 還 還 還 還 還	
四 罒 咢 罗 罘 罘 罘 罘 還 還			
還			

| 可 kě (43) but | 可 | 可 可 可 可 可 可 | |
| 一 口 可 | | | |

| 們 men (12) *(plural suffix) | 們 们 | 們 們 們 們 們 | |
| 亻 們 | | | |

點	diǎn (93) dot; o'clock	點	點	點	點	點	點
	點 点						
丶	冂	冂	四	四	甲	甲	里	黑	黑丶
黑丶	點						

鐘 see page 135	zhōng (699) clock	鐘	鐘	鐘	鐘	鐘	鐘
	鐘 钟						
金	金	釒	釒	釒亠	釒立	釒立	釒音	釒音	釒音
鐘	鐘	鐘					

半	bàn (307) half	半	半	半	半	半	半
	半						
丶	丷	丷	兰	半			

上	shàng (15) above; top	上	上	上	上	上	上
	上						
丨	卜	上					

見	jiàn (101) to see			見	見	見	見	見	見
	見	见							
目	貝	見							

再	zài (219) again			再	再	再	再	再	再
	再								
一	厂	厅	丙	丙	再				

白	bái (230) white			白	白	白	白	白	白
	白								
丿	白								

Dialogue II

	xiàn (83) now	現 現 現 現 現 現					
現	現 現						
王 現							

	zài (7) (to be) at	在 在 在 在 在 在					
在	在						
一 ナ 冇 存 存 在							

	kè (†) quarter hour	刻 刻 刻 刻 刻 刻					
刻	刻						
亥 刻							

	míng (160) bright	明 明 明 明 明 明					
明	明						
日 明							

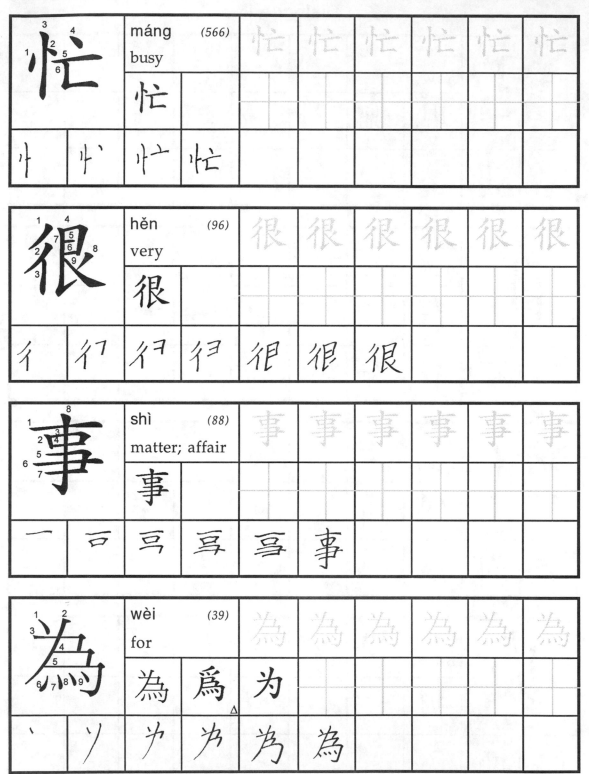

(Note: A different font is used here because the main font displays the printing form.)

因	yīn (190) because	因	因	因	因	因	因
	因						
丨	冂	因	因				

同	tóng (66) same	同	同	同	同	同	同
	同						
冂	冃	同					

認	rèn (294) to recognize	認	認	認	認	認	認
	認 认						
言	訒	訒	認				

識	shí (315) to recognize	識	識	識	識	識	識
see page 135	識 识						
言	訒	語	識	識	識		

Dialogue I

週	zhōu (690) week	週	週	週	週	週	週
	週 周						
ノ	刀	月	用	用	周	週	

末	mò (†) end	末	末	末	末	末	末
	末						
一	二	丰	才	末			

打	dǎ (136) to hit; to strike	打	打	打	打	打	
	打						
扌	扩	打					

球	qiú (605) ball	球	球	球	球	球	球
	球						
王	玗	玎	封	玳	球	球	球

看	kàn (41) to watch; to look	看	看	看	看	看
	看					
一	㇐	三	手	看		

(Please note that the first stroke goes down from right to left.)

電	diàn (77) electric	電	電	電	電	電	電
	電	电					
雨	雨	雷	雷	雷	電		

視	shì (612) vision	視	視	視	視	視	視
	視	视					
礻	視						

唱	chàng (679) to sing	唱	唱	唱	唱	唱	唱
	唱						
口	口日	唱					

歌	gē (725) song	歌	歌	歌	歌	歌	歌
	歌						
哥	歌						

跳	tiào (611) to jump	跳	跳	跳	跳	跳	跳
	跳						
足	趴	趴	趴	趴	跳	跳	

舞	wǔ (954) to dance; dance	舞	舞	舞	舞	舞	
	舞						
丿	𠂉	仁	𠂤	无	无	细	無	無	舞
舞	舞	舞	舞				

聽	tīng (161) to listen	聽	聽	聽	聽	聽	聽
	聽	听					
一	丁	丌	月	耳	耳	耳艹	耹	耹
聽							

音	yīn (487) sound	音	音	音	音	音	音
	音						
丶	亠	立	立	立	音		

樂	yuè / lè (713) music/happy	樂	樂	樂	樂	樂	樂
	樂	乐					
白	幼	丝	樂				

對	duì (60) correct; right; toward	對	對	對	對	對	
	對	对					
㇑	㇚	业	业	业	业	业	丵	丵	對
對							

				時	時	時	時	時	時
時	shí (34) time								
	時	时							
日	日一	日十	旪	時					

				候	候	候	候	候	候
候	hòu (147) to wait								
	候								
亻	亻	俨	俨	俨	俨	候	候		

				書	書	書	書	書	書
書	shū (238) book								
	書	书							
乛	乛	彐	彐	彐	聿	書			

				影	影	影	影	影	影
影	yǐng (399) shadow								
	影								
日	早	旦	昌	景	景	影	影		

常	cháng (202) often	常	常	常	常	常	常
	常						
丨	丶	⺌	⺌	当	告	告	告	常

去	qù (29) to go	去	去	去	去	去	去
	去						
一	十	土	去	去

外	wài (141) outside	外	外	外	外	外	外
	外						
夕	夘	外

客	kè (532) guest	客	客	客	客	客	客
	客						
宀	宀	宀	客	客

昨	zuó (†) yesterday	昨	昨	昨	昨	昨	昨
	昨						
日	昨						

所	suǒ (127) *so; place	所	所	所	所	所	所
	所	所					
´	厂	戶	戶	戶	所	所	所

以	yǐ (44) with	以	以	以	以	以	以
	以						
㇄	㇇	以	以				

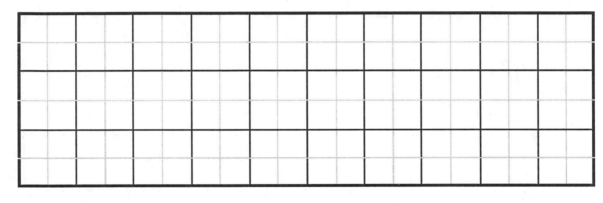

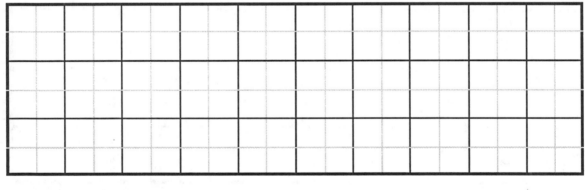

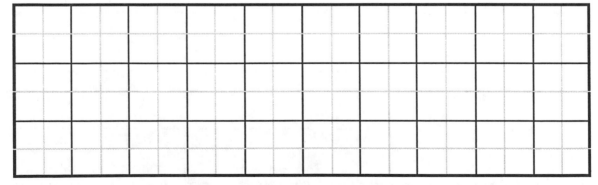

Dialogue II

久	jiǔ (621) a long time	久	久	久	久	久	久
	久						
ノ	夕	久					

錯	cuò (429) wrong	錯	錯	錯	錯	錯	錯
	錯	错					
金	金	釒	釒	釒	錯		

想	xiǎng (69) to think	想	想	想	想	想	想
	想						
木	相	想					

覺	jué / jiào (302) to feel / *sleep	覺	覺	覺	覺	覺	覺
	覺	觉					
臼	覺						

		dé (28) to get		得	得	得	得	得	得
得		得							
亻	彳	徂	得						

		yì (122) meaning		意	意	意	意	意	意
意		意							
立	音	意							

		sī (227) to think		思	思	思	思	思	思
思		思							
田	思								

		zhǐ (85) only		只	只	只	只	只	只
只		只							
口	叧	只							

睡	shuì (506) to sleep	睡	睡	睡	睡	睡	睡
	睡						
目	目	目	盯	盱	眜	眪	睡

(Please note that stroke 6 goes down from right to left.)

算	suàn (334) to calculate	算	算	算	算	算	算
	算						
ノ	ト	大	竹	竹	笪	笪	算	算

找	zhǎo (361) to look for	找	找	找	找	找	找
	找						
扌	找						

别	bié (167) other	别	别	别	别	别	别
	别	别					
口	号	另	别				

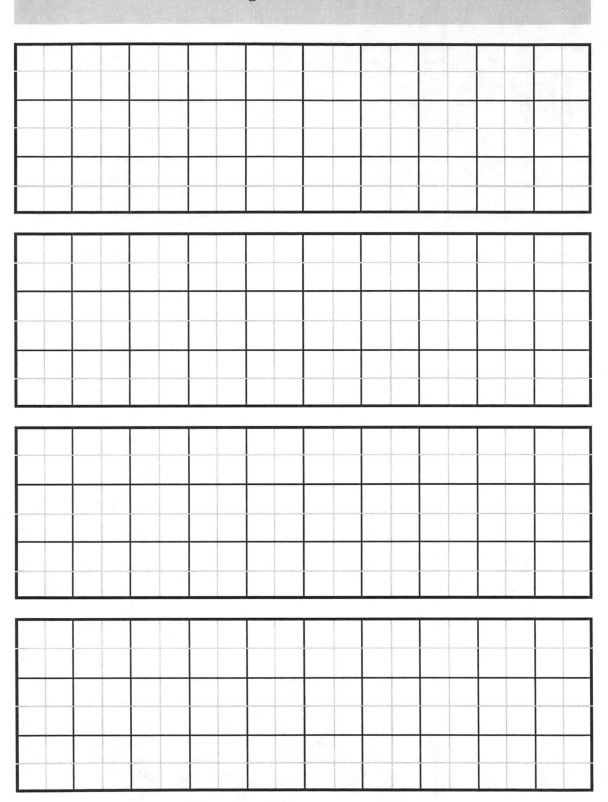

Dialogue I

呀	ya (267) P	呀	呀	呀	呀	呀	呀
	呀						
口	口⁻	叮	吘	呀			

進	jìn (81) to enter	進	進	進	進	進	進
	進 进						
隹 進							

快	kuài (223) fast; quick(ly)	快	快	快	快	快	快
	快						
忄 忄丁 忄工 快 快							

來	lái (13) to come	來	來	來	來	來	來
	來 来						
一 十 才 才 木 来 來 來							

介	jiè (†) between 介	人	亻	介	介	介	介	介	介	介
紹	shào (†) carry on 紹 绍	幺	紀	紹	紹	紹	紹	紹	紹	紹
下	xià (36) below; under 下	一	丁	下	下	下	下	下	下	下
興	xìng (†) mood; interest 興 兴	ノ	亻	𠂊	𠂊	𦉪	𦉰	𦉰	𦉰	𦉰
		𦉰	興	興	興					

漂	piào (t) *pretty	漂	漂	漂	漂	漂	漂
	漂						
氵	氵	汩	沪	沪	沪	酒	酒	漂	漂

亮	liàng (538) bright	亮	亮	亮	亮	亮	亮
	亮	亮					
亠	亠	亮	亮				

坐	zuò (371) to sit	坐	坐	坐	坐	坐	坐
	坐						
人	人人	坐	坐	坐			

哪	nǎ / něi (275) QW; which	哪	哪	哪	哪	哪	哪
	哪						
口	哪						

工	gōng (55) craft	工	工	工	工	工	工
	工						
工							

作	zuò (214) to work; to do	作	作	作	作	作	
	作						
亻	作						

校	xiào (636) school	校	校	校	校	校	校
	校						
木	术	杧	柠	柼	栌	校	

喝	hē (720) to drink	喝	喝	喝	喝	喝	喝
	喝						
口	口甲	口曷	喝	喝	喝		

茶	chá (985) tea	茶	茶	茶	茶	茶	茶
	茶	茶					
十	艹	艾	苎	苶	茶	茶	

咖	kā *coffee	咖	咖	咖	咖	咖	咖
	咖						
口	叻	咖					

啡	fēi *coffee	啡	啡	啡	啡	啡	啡
	啡						
口	叮	叭	叶	叩	呖	啡	啡	啡

啤	pí *beer	啤	啤	啤	啤	啤	啤
	啤						
口	叮	叩	听	咱	咱	啤	哩	啤

酒	jiǔ (858) wine 酒	酒	酒	酒	酒	酒	酒
氵	氵	汀	沂	沔	沔	酒	

吧	ba (175) P 吧	吧	吧	吧	吧	吧	吧
口	吧						

要	yào (25) to want 要	要	要	要	要	要	要
一	一	一	西	西	西	要	

杯	bēi (†) cup; glass 杯	杯	杯	杯	杯	杯	杯
木	杯						

起	qǐ (47) to rise		起	起	起	起	起	起
	起							
十	土	圥	圥	赱	走	起	起	起

給	gěi (114) to give		給	給	給	給	給	給
	給	给						
幺	幻	絲	給					

水	shuǐ (102) water		水	水	水	水	水	水
	水							
水								

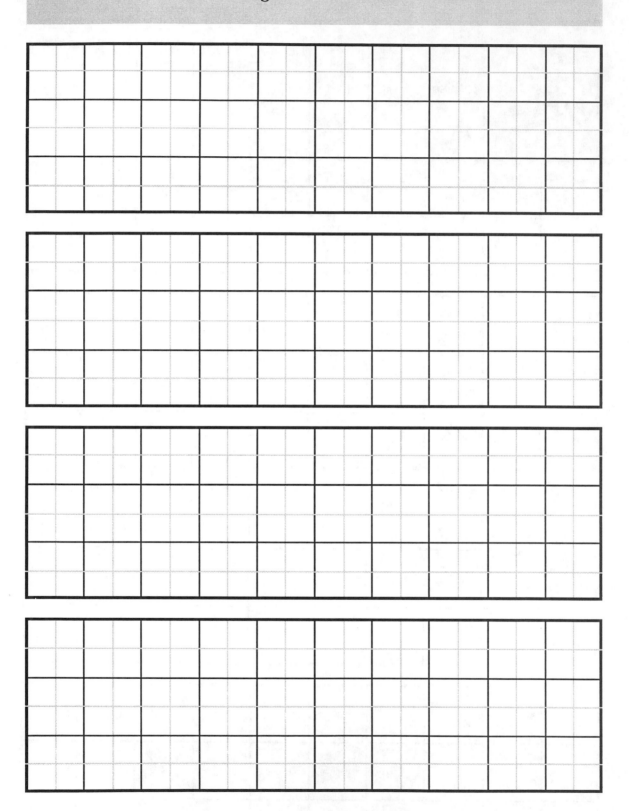

Dialogue II

玩	wán (970) to have a visit; to play			玩	玩	玩	玩	玩
	玩							
王	玉	玩						

圖 see page 135	tú (7) drawing			圖	圖	圖	圖	圖	圖
	圖	图							
丨	冂	冋	冋	囝	冏	昂	圖	圖	圖

館	guǎn (938) accomodations			館	館	館	館	館
	館	馆						
食	飠	飠	飠	飠	館	館		

瓶	píng (†) bottle			瓶	瓶	瓶	瓶	瓶	瓶
	瓶								
丶	丷	丷	丷	半	并	并	瓶	瓶	瓶

聊	liáo (†) to chat	聊	聊	聊	聊	聊	聊
	聊						
耳	耳	耳	耶	聊	聊		

才	cái (162) not until	才	才	才	才	才	才
	才						
一	十	才					

回	huí (108) to return	回	回	回	回	回	回
	回						
丨	冂	冋	回				

Dialogue I

話	huà (137) speech	話	話	話	話	話	話
	話 话						
言	言	訁	訐	話			

喂	wèi (†) Hello!; Hey!	喂	喂	喂	喂	喂	喂
	喂						
口	叩	嘊	哩	喂	喂		

就	jiù (19) then	就	就	就	就	就	就
	就						
亠	古	京	京	就	就	就	

位	wèi (†) M (polite)	位	位	位	位	位	位
	位						
亻	亻'	仁	仃	位	位		

午	wǔ (882) noon	午	午	午	午	午	午
	午						
ノ 〳 〥 午							

間	jiān (156) M (for rooms)	間	間	間	間	間	
	間 间						
門 間							

題	tí (224) topic; question	題	題	題	題	題	
	題 题						
是 是 是 題							

開	kāi (94) to open; to hold	開	開	開	開	開	
	開 开						
門 門 門 閂 開							

會 see page 135	huì (32) to meet	會	會	會	會	會	會
	會 会						
人	仒	仐	合	佘	侖	侖	侖	會

節	jié (555) M (for classes)	節	節	節	節	節	
	節 节						
⺮	⺮⺮	竻	竻	筲	管	節	節

課	kè (762) class; lesson	課	課	課	課	課	課
	課 课						
言	言	訂	訂	訶	誀	評	課	課

級	jí (172) level; rank	級	級	級	級	級	級
	級 级						
糸	刹	紅	紨	級			

考	kǎo (767) to give or take a test	考	考	考	考	考
	考 考					
一	十	土	尹	尹	考	

試	shì (701) to try; to test	試	試	試	試	試	試
	試 试					
言	言	訁	訂	訌	試	試

後	hòu (73) after; rear	後	後	後	後	後	後
	後 后					
彳	彳	徉	移	後		

空	kòng (340) free time	空	空	空	空	空	空
	空					
宀	宁	空	空			

方	fāng (96) square	方	方	方	方	方	方
	方						
丶	一	亠	方				

便	biàn / pián (282) convenient / *cheap	便	便	便	便	便	
	便						
亻	亻	伍	便	便			

到	dào (22) to go to; to arrive	到	到	到	到	到	
	到						
一	工	云	至	到			

辦	bàn (313) to manage	辦	辦	辦	辦	辦	辦
	辦	办					
丶	亠	辛	产	立	辛	辛	勃	勃	勃
勃	勃	辦	辦				

公	gōng (259) public	公	公	公	公	公	公
	公						
八	公	公					

室	shì (669) room	室	室	室	室	室	室
	室						
宀	宀	宀	宀	室	室	室	

行	xíng (99) be all right; OK	行	行	行	行	行	
	行						
彳	彳	彳	行				

等	děng (35) to wait	等	等	等	等	等	等
	等						
竹	竺	等					

氣	qì (11) air	氣	氣	氣	氣	氣	氣
	氣 气						
ノ	ト	ᅡ	气	气	氕	気	氣 氣 氣

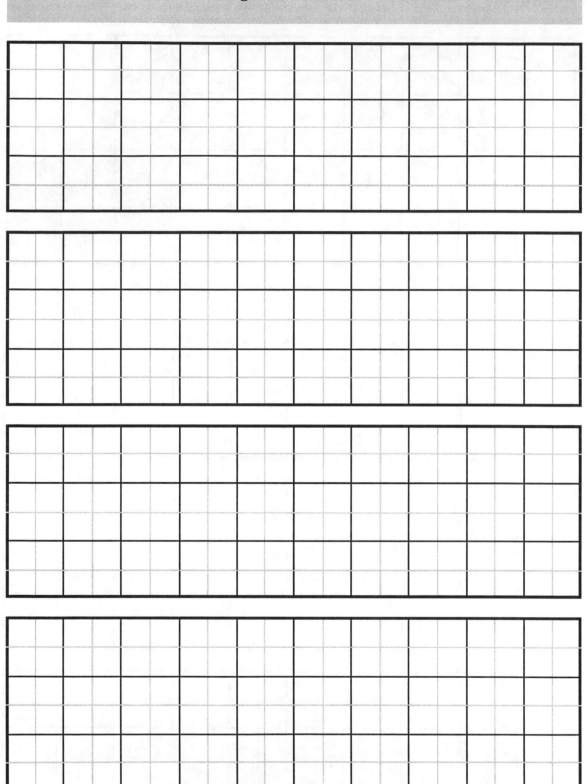

Dialogue II

	bāng (536) to help	幫	幫	幫	幫	幫	幫
幫 see page 136	幫 帮						
	土	圭	封	幇	幇	幫	幫

	liàn (950) to drill	練	練	練	練	練	練
練 see page 136	練 练						
	糸	糸	紅	約	紡	緬	緬	紳	練	練

	xí (417) to practice	習	習	習	習	習	習
習	習 习						
	习	习	习	羽	羽	羽	習

| 說 shuō (21) to speak | 説 | 说 | 説 説 説 説 説 説 | | | | | |
| 言 | 言 | 言 | 訁 | 訜 | 說 | | | |

| 啊 a (254) P | 啊 | | 啊 啊 啊 啊 啊 啊 | | | | | |
| 口 | 呵 | 啊 | | | | | | |

| 但 dàn (150) but | 但 | | 但 但 但 但 但 但 | | | | | |
| 亻 | 佀 | 但 | | | | | | |

| 知 zhī (131) to know | 知 | | 知 知 知 知 知 知 | | | | | |
| 丿 | 亇 | 乍 | 矢 | 矢 | 知 | | | |

道	dào (78) path; way	道	道	道	道	道	道
	道						
丶	丷	丷	丷	首	道		

Dialogue I

跟	gēn (247) with; to follow; and	跟	跟	跟	跟	跟
	跟					
𧾷	跟						

助	zhù (632) to assist	助	助	助	助	助	助
	助					
且	助						

復	fù (525) duplicate	復	復	復	復	復	復
	復	复				
彳	彳	彳	復	復			

寫	xiě (317) to write	寫	寫	寫	寫	寫	寫
	寫	写				
宀	宀	宀	寫	寫			

慢	màn (657) slow	慢	慢	慢	慢	慢	慢
	慢						
小	忄	愠	慢				

教	jiāo (244) to teach	教	教	教	教	教	教
	教 教 △						
一	十	土	少	耂	耂	孝	教
							教

筆	bǐ (775) pen	筆	筆	筆	筆	筆	筆
	筆 笔						
竹	笁	笁	筀	筆			

難	nán (285) difficult *see page 136*	難	難	難	難	難	難
	難 难						
一	十	廿	苩	莒	莒	茣	莫
							難

裡	lǐ (26) inside	裡	裡	裡	裡	裡	裡
	裡 裏 里 △						
礻 祀 袒 袒 裡							

第	dì (211) (ordinal prefix)	第	第	第	第	第	
	第						
竹 第							

預	yù (892) to prepare	預	預	預	預	預	預
	預 预						
ㄱ マ 予 予 予 予 予 預							

語	yǔ (706) language	語	語	語	語	語	語
	語 语						
言 語 語							

法	fǎ (142) method; way	法	法	法	法	法	法
	法						
氵	法						

容	róng (421) hold; contain; allow	容	容	容	容	容	
	容						
宀	宀	宛	容				

易	yì (582) easy	易	易	易	易	易	易
	易						
日	日	吊	易	易			

懂	dǒng (269) to understand	懂	懂	懂	懂	懂	
	懂	懂					
忄	忄艹	忄艹	忄芷	愭	懂	懂	懂

詞	cí (t) word	詞	詞	詞	詞	詞	詞	詞
	詞 词							
言 訂 訂 詞								

漢	hàn (t) Chinese	漢	漢	漢	漢	漢	漢	漢
	漢 汉							
氵 漢								

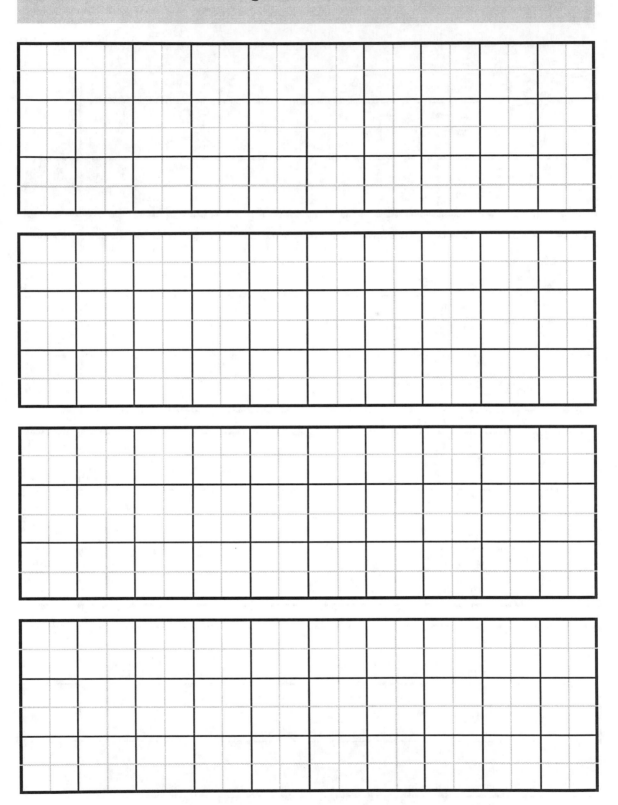

Dialogue II

平	píng (232) level; even	平	平	平	平	平	平
	平						
一	ㄥ	ㄗ	平	平			

早	zǎo (344) early	早	早	早	早	早	早
	早						
日	早						

夜	yè (405) night	夜	夜	夜	夜	夜	夜
	夜						
丶	一	亠	疒	庈	夜	夜	

功	gōng (681) skill	功	功	功	功	功	功
	功						
工	功						

真	zhēn (159) true; real(ly)	真	真	真	真	真	真
	真	眞 △					
一	十	广	疒	疒	肎	肎	直 真 真

始	shǐ (548) to begin	始	始	始	始	始	始
	始						
女	女	始					

唸	niàn (620) to read	唸	唸	唸	唸	唸	唸
	唸	念					
口	吟	唸					

錄	lù (†) to record	錄	錄	錄	錄	錄	錄
	錄	录					
金	釒	釒	釒	釒	釒	錄	錄 錄

帥	shuài (†) handsome; smart	帥	帥	帥	帥	帥
	帥 帅					
丿	亻	亽	卩	臼	臼	自	師	帥

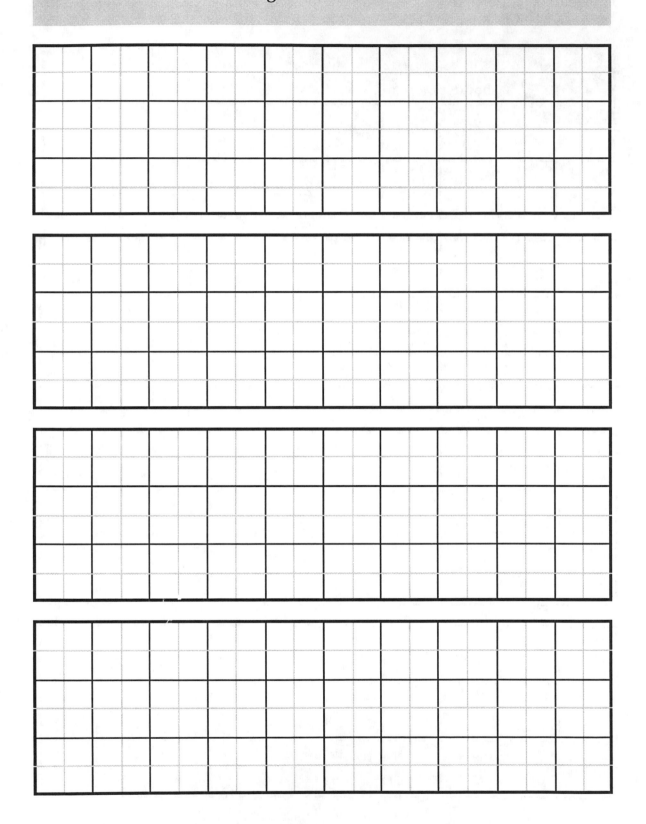

Dialogue I

篇	piān (f) M (for articles)	篇	篇	篇	篇	篇
	篇					
⺮	⺮	乍	竻	竻	竻	篙	篙	篇	篇

記	jì (289) record	記	記	記	記	記	記
	記	记					
言	訂	訂	記				

床	chuáng (682) bed	床	床	床	床	床	床
	床	牀					
、	广	广	床				

洗	xǐ (860) to wash	洗	洗	洗	洗	洗	洗
	洗						
氵	氵	氵	汁	沣	浐	洗	

	zǎo (†) bath		澡	澡	澡	澡	澡	澡
澡	澡							
氵	汈	沼	澡	澡				

	biān (140) side		邊	邊	邊	邊	邊	
邊 *see page 136*	邊	边						
丿	自	自	自	鳥	鳥	鳥	鳥	粵
粵	邊							

	fā (64) to emit; to issue		發	發	發	發	發	
發	發	发						
ㄋ	ㄋ	癶	癶	癶	弢	發		

	nǎo (600) brain		腦	腦	腦	腦	腦	腦
腦	腦	脑						
月	肝	肝	肝	肸	肸	腦	腦	腦

餐	cān (†) meal 餐		餐	餐	餐	餐	餐	餐
㇔	㇡	歺	歺又	歺又	炊	炊	餐	餐
餐	餐	餐						

廳 see page 136	tīng (†) hall 廳 厅		廳	廳	廳	廳	廳	廳
广	廳							

報	bào (333) newspaper 報 报		報	報	報	報	報	報
一	十	土	圥	圥	坴	坴	幸	報	報
報								

宿	sù (†) to stay 宿		宿	宿	宿	宿	宿	宿
宀	宀	宁	宿					

舍	shè　　(†) house	舍	舍	舍	舍	舍	舍
	舍						
人	人	今	今	舍			

正	zhèng　　(†) just	正	正	正	正	正	正
	正						
一	丁	下	疒	正			

前	qián　　(91) front; before	前	前	前	前	前	前
	前						
丶	丷	丷	肯	前			

告	gào　　(346) to tell; to inform	告	告	告	告	告	
	告						
丿	丷	屮	牛	告			

訴	sù (545) to tell; to relate	訴	訴	訴	訴	訴
	訴 诉					
言 訴 訴						

已	yǐ (171) already	己	己	己	己	己
	已					
フ コ 己						

經	jīng (76) pass through	經	經	經	經	經
	經 经					
糸 糸 糸 紅 絲 經						

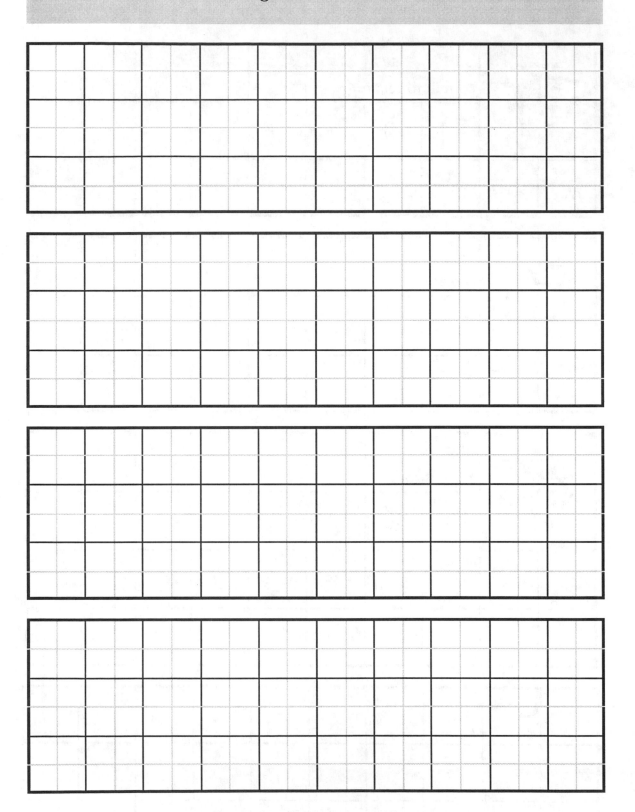

Dialogue II

			fēng (689) M (for letters)	封	封	封	封	封	封
	封		封						
土	圭	封							

		fēng	xìn (318) letter	信	信	信	信	信	信
	信		信						
亻	信								

			zuì (174) (superalative); most	最	最	最	最	最	
	最		最						
日	取	最							

			jìn (414) near	近	近	近	近	近	近
	近		近						
斤	近								

除	chú (562) except		除	除	除	除	除	除
	除							
阝	阝人	阝八	阥	除	除	除		

專	zhuān (519) special		專	專	專	專	專	專
	專	专						
一	百	甫	重	重	專			

業	yè (†) occupation; profession		業	業	業	業	業	
	業	业						
业	业	业	业	苎	芏	芏	芏	業

慣	guàn (†) to be used to		慣	慣	慣	慣	慣	慣
	慣	惯						
忄	忄	忄	忄	忄	慣			

清	qīng (381) clear; clean	清	清	清	清	清	清
	清						
氵	清						

楚	chǔ (907) clear; neat	楚	楚	楚	楚	楚	楚
	楚						
木	林	梺	梺	梺	梺	楚	

步	bù (314) step	步	步	步	步	步	步
	步						
㇑	㇠	止	止	步	步	步	

希	xī (818) hope	希	希	希	希	希	希
	希						
ノ	乂	乆	希				

望	wàng (298) hope; expect	望	望	望	望	望	望
	望	望					
丶	亠	亡	亡'	功	功	功	望	望
望							

能	néng (52) to be able	能	能	能	能	能	能
	能						
ㄥ	ㄥ	育	育	能	能	能		

用	yòng (59) to use	用	用	用	用	用	用
	用						
丿	冂	月	月	用			

笑	xiào (250) to laugh	笑	笑	笑	笑	笑	笑
	笑						
竹	竹	竺	笑	笑			

	zhù (†) to wish	祝	祝	祝	祝	祝	祝
祝	祝						
丶	㇀	㇏	㇈	礻	初	初	祝

Dialogue I

買	mǎi (460) to buy	買	買	買	買	買	買
	買 买						
四 買							

東	dōng (234) east	東	東	東	東	東	東
	東 东						
一 亡 東 東 東							

西	xī (225) west	西	西	西	西	西	西
	西						
一 一 一 两 西 西							

售	shòu (†) to sell	售	售	售	售	售	售
	售						
隹 售							

貨	huò (773) merchandise	貨	貨	貨	貨	貨	貨
	貨 货						
亻 化 貨							

員	yuán (200) personnel	員	員	員	員	員	員
	員 员						
口 員							

衣	yī (473) clothing	衣	衣	衣	衣	衣	衣
	衣						
丶 亠 ㇉ 𧘇 衣 衣							

服	fú (375) clothing	服	服	服	服	服	服
	服						
月 服							

件	jiàn (311) M (for items)	件	件	件	件	件	件	件
	件							
亻	亻	亻	仁	件				

襯 see page 136	chèn (†) lining	襯	襯	襯	襯	襯	襯	襯
	襯	衬						
衤	衤	衤	衤	衤	衤	衤	衤	襯
襯								

衫	shān (†) shirt	衫	衫	衫	衫	衫	衫	衫
	衫							
衤	衤	衫	衫					

顏	yán (†) face; countenance	顏	顏	顏	顏	顏	顏	顏
	顏	颜						
丶	亠	立	文	文	产	声	彦	彦	顏

色	sè (287) color	色	色	色	色	色	色
	色						
ノ	ク	色					

黄	huáng (638) yellow	黄	黄	黄	黄	黄	黄
	黄	黄△					
一	十	艹	艹	芒	苦	昔	苗	苗	黄
黄							

紅	hóng (352) red	紅	紅	紅	紅	紅	紅
	紅	紅					
纟	紅						

穿	chuān (539) to wear	穿	穿	穿	穿	穿	穿
	穿						
穴	空	空	穿	穿			

條	tiáo (213)		條	條	條	條	條
	M (for long objects)						
	條	条					
亻	亻	伥	伅	伀	攸	條		

褲	kù (†)		褲	褲	褲	褲	褲	褲
	pants							
see page 137	褲	褲					
衤	衤	衤	裇	裇	褲		

宜	yí (†)		宜	宜	宜	宜	宜
	suitable; *cheap						
	宜						
宀	宜						

付	fù (†)		付	付	付	付	付	付
	to pay							
	付							
亻	付							

錢	qián (398) money	錢	錢	錢	錢	錢	錢
	錢	钱					
金	金	金	鉖	鉖	鉖	錢	錢	錢

共	gòng (283) altogether	共	共	共	共	共	共
	共						
一	十	艹	芏	共	共			

少	shǎo (192) few	少	少	少	少	少	少
	少						
小	少						

塊	kuài (403) piece; dollar	塊	塊	塊	塊	塊	塊
	塊	块					
士	圠	坤	坤	塊	塊	塊	

毛	máo (531) hair; dime	毛	毛	毛	毛	毛	毛
	毛						
ノ 二 三 毛							

分	fēn (90) penny; minute	分	分	分	分	分	
	分						
八 分							

百	bǎi (233) hundred	百	百	百	百	百	百
	百						
一 丁 百							

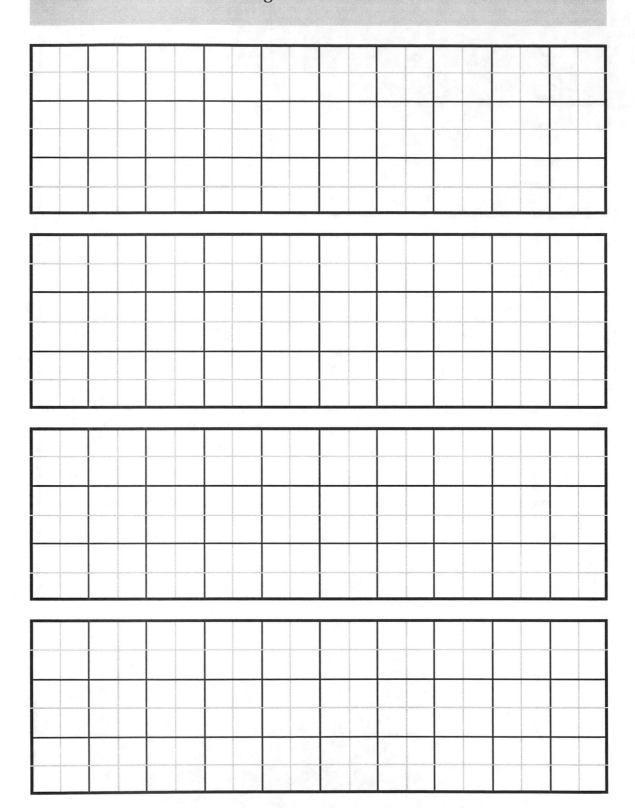

Dialogue II

雙	shuāng (729) M; pair	雙	雙	雙	雙	雙	雙
	雙	双					
隹	雔	雙					

鞋	xié (901) shoe	鞋	鞋	鞋	鞋	鞋	鞋
	鞋						
艹	苫	苴	革	鞋	鞋		

換	huàn (745) to (ex)change	換	換	換	換	換	換
	換	換					
扌	扌	扩	护	护	换	换	搶	換	換

黑	hēi (438) black	黑	黑	黑	黑	黑	黑
	黑						
丶	丨	冂	四	四	甲	里	黑

雖	suí (603) though	雖	雖	雖	雖	雖	雖
	雖	虽					
口	吕	虽	虽	虽	雖		

然	rán (84) like that; so	然	然	然	然	然	然
	然						
夕	外	然	然				

合	hé (215) to suit; to agree	合	合	合	合	合
	合					
人	合	合				

適	shì (757) to suit; to fit	適	適	適	適	適	適
	適 适						
、	宀	宀	宀	户	冇	矞	商	商	適

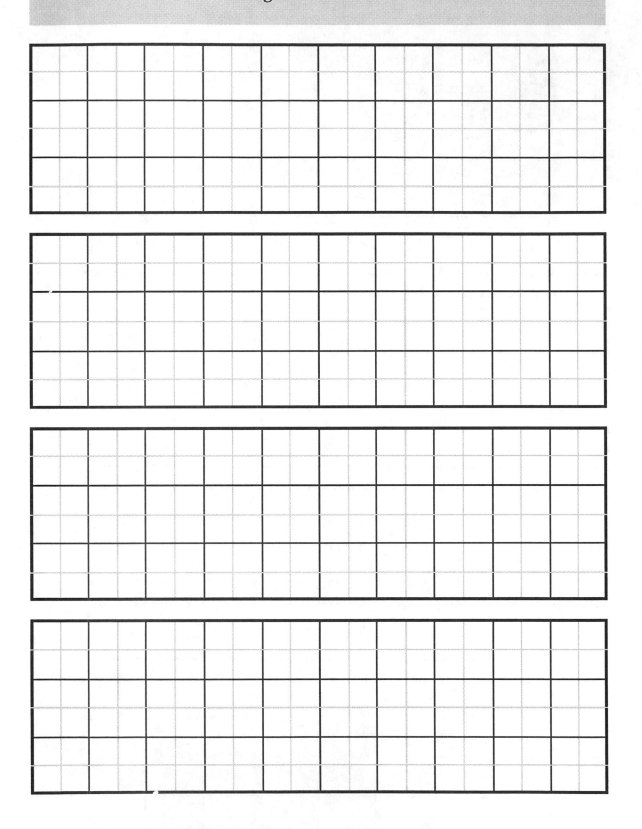

Dialogue I

比	bǐ (206) to compare	比	比	比	比	比	比
	比						
´	ヒ	ヒ	比				

雨	yǔ (542) rain	雨	雨	雨	雨	雨	雨
	雨						
一	冂	冂	而	而	雨	雨	雨

更	gèng (260) even more	更	更	更	更	更	更
	更						
一	百	更	更				

而	ér (95) and; in addition	而	而	而	而	而	
	而						
一	丆	广	丙	而	而		

且	qiě (355) for the time being	且	且	且	且	且
	且					
丨	冂	冃	月	且		

暖	nuǎn (†) warm	暖	暖	暖	暖	暖	暖
	暖						
日	日	旷	旷	旷	晔	晔	暖	暖

約	yuē (568) to make an appointment	約	約	約	約
	約	约			
糸	糸	約	約		

園	yuán (898) garden	園	園	園	園	園	園
	園	园					
丨	冂	冂	圊	圊	園	園	園

葉	yè (777) leaf	葉	葉	葉	葉	葉	葉
	葉	叶					
艹	艹	艹	艹	艹	苎	葉	

像	xiàng (†) image; picture	像	像	像	像	像	
	像						
亻	伫	伫	伖	伖	伖	伊	傻	像
像	像						

海	hǎi (348) sea	海	海	海	海	海	海
	海						
氵	氵	汽	海	海	海	海	

Dialogue II

糟 see page 137	zāo (†) messy; in a mess			糟	糟	糟	糟	糟
	糟							
丶	丷	丷	半	半	米	米	米	粐	粐
粐	糟	糟	糟					

糕	gāo (†) cake			糕	糕	糕	糕	糕	糕
	糕							
米	糕	糕						

又	yòu (65) again			又	又	又	又	又	又
	又							
ㄱ	又							

剛	gāng (415) just now	剛	剛	剛	剛	剛	剛
	剛 刚						
丨	冂	冂	罓	岡	冈	岡	岡	剛

出	chū (35) to go out	出	出	出	出	出	出
	出						
乚	屮	屮	出	出			

熱	rè (319) hot	熱	熱	熱	熱	熱	熱
	熱 热						
土	扌	夫	坴	刦	執	執	熱

舒	shū (†) stretch	舒	舒	舒	舒	舒	舒
	舒						
人	亼	今	全	舍	舍	舍	舒	舒

	xià (†) summer	夏	夏	夏	夏	夏	夏
夏	夏						
一	丁	百	頁	夏			

	liáng (†) cool	涼	涼	涼	涼	涼	涼
涼	涼	涼					
氵	冫	氵	泸	涼			

	chūn (736) spring	春	春	春	春	春	春
春	春						
一	二	三	夫	夫	春		

	dōng (†) winter	冬	冬	冬	冬	冬	冬
冬	冬						
丿	夕	夂	冬	冬			

冷	lěng (587) cold	冷	冷	冷	冷	冷	冷
	冷						
丶	冫	冫	冫	冷	冷		

悶	mēn (†) stuffy	悶	悶	悶	悶	悶	悶
	悶	闷					
尸	門	悶					

次	cì (210) M (for occurrences)	次	次	次	次	次	
	次						
冫	冫	次					

秋	qiū (†) autumn; fall	秋	秋	秋	秋	秋	秋
	秋						
丿	禾	秋					

台	tái (526) platform; stage	台	台	台	台	台
台	臺 △					
ㄥ	ㄙ	台					

北	běi (464) north	北	北	北	北	北	北
北						
丨	十	土	北				

灣 see page 137	wān (†) strait; bay	灣	灣	灣	灣	灣
灣	湾					
氵	氵言	灤	灤	灣			

Dialogue I

	hán (†) winter	寒	寒	寒	寒	寒	寒
寒	寒						
宀	宀	宀	宰	宰	宲	宲	寒	寒	寒

	jià (831) vacation	假	假	假	假	假	假
假	假						
亻	伫	伫	伊	伊	伊	伊	伊	假

	fēi (357) to fly	飛	飛	飛	飛	飛	飛
飛	飞	飛	飞				
乙	飞	飞	飞	飛	飛	飛	飛	飛

	jī (125) machine	機	機	機	機	機	機
機	机						
木	機						

票	piào ticket (†)	票	票	票	票	票	票
	票						
西	票						

場	chǎng (364) field	場	場	場	場	場	場
	場	场					
土	圫	坦	坥	场	場	場	

汽	qì (507) steam; gas	汽	汽	汽	汽	汽	汽
	汽						
氵	氵	氵	汽	汽			

車	chē (178) car; vehicle	車	車	車	車	車	車
	車	车					
一	百	亘	車				

或	huò (331) or	或	或	或	或	或	或
	或						
一	口	豆	或	或	或		

者	zhě (258) P	者	者	者	者	者	者
	者						
土	耂	者					

地	dì (16) ground	地	地	地	地	地	地
	地						
圡	地						

鐵 see page 137	tiě (439) iron	鐵	鐵	鐵	鐵	鐵	鐵
	鐵 铁						
金	金	釒	鈝	鋯	鐱	鐵	鐵	鐵

走	zǒu (104) to walk	走	走	走	走	走	走	走
		走						
土	卡	卡	走	走				

站	zhàn (338) to stand; station	站	站	站	站	站
		站				
丶	亠	亠	立	立	刘	北	站	

綠	lǜ (851) green	錄	錄	錄	錄	錄	錄
		綠	绿				
幺	糸	糸	絽	綧	綧	綧	綠	綠

線	xiàn (263) line; route	線	線	線	線	線	線
		線	线				
幺	紀	線				

藍	lán (†) blue	藍	藍	藍	藍	藍	藍
	藍 蓝						
艹	艹	艹	艹	艹	艹	藍	藍	藍	藍
蓝	藍	藍	藍	藍					

麻	má (†) hemp	麻	麻	麻	麻	麻	麻
	麻						
广	床	麻					

煩	fán (†) to trouble	煩	煩	煩	煩	煩	煩
	煩 烦						
丶	丷	少	火	灯	煩	煩	

租	zū (†) to rent	租	租	租	租	租	租
	租						
禾	租						

送	sòng (469) to deliver; to see off; to send	送	送	送	送
	送				

| 、 | ㇏ | 丷 | 丷 | 关 | 关 | 送 | | | |

Dialogue II

	guò (38) to pass	過	過	過	過	過	過
過	過 过						
	一 丨 冂 丹 冎 咼 咼 過						

	ràng (379) to let; to allow	讓	讓	讓	讓	讓	
讓 *see page 137*	讓 让						
言 言 訂 訠 諒 諒 諄 諄 譲 譲							
讓 讓 讓							

	huā (240) flower; to spend	花	花	花	花	花	
花	花 花						
艹 艹 花							

	měi (306) every; each	每	每	每	每	每	每
每	每						
丿 每							

	sù (503) speed	速	速	速	速	速	速
速	速						
一	一 口	申	束	束	速		

	lù (165) road; way	路	路	路	路	路	路
路	路						
𧾷	𧾷	趵	跋	路			

	jǐn (412) tense; tight	緊	緊	緊	緊	緊	緊
緊	緊 緊						
臣	臤	堅	緊				

	zì (63) self; from	自	自	自	自	自	自
自	自						
丿	自						

己	jǐ (130) self	己		己	己	己	己	己	己
	己								
ㄱ	ㄱ	己							

新	xīn (181) new	新		新	新	新	新	新	新
	新								
立	亲	新							

禮	lǐ (†) ceremony	禮	礼	禮	禮	禮	禮	禮	禮
礻	礻	礻	礻	神	褆	褆	襠	禧	禮
襠	禮								

物	wù (132) thing	物		物	物	物	物	物	物
	物								
ノ	㇄	牛	牛	物					

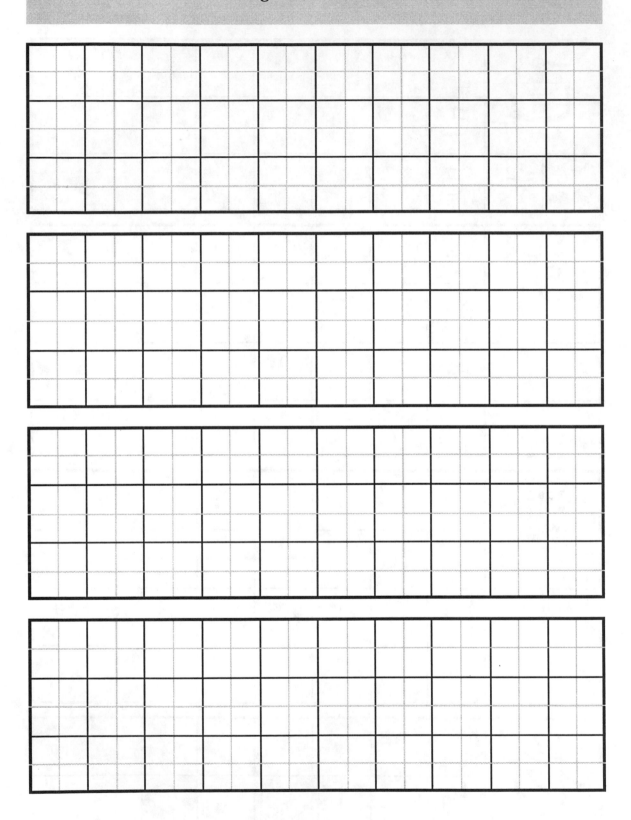

INDICES

Enlarged Characters for Easier Viewing

Lesson 2	Lesson 3	Lesson 3
醫	歡	鐘
see page 33	*see page 40*	*see page 41*
yī	huān	zhōng

Lesson 3	Lesson 5	Lesson 6
識	圖	會
see page 45	*see page 67*	*see page 71*
shí	tú	huì

Lesson 6	Lesson 6	Lesson 7
幫	練	難
see page 77	*see page 77*	*see page 82*
bāng	liàn	nán

Lesson 8	Lesson 8	Lesson 9
邊	廳	襯
see page 92	*see page 93*	*see page 105*
biān	tīng	chèn

Lesson 9	Lesson 10	Lesson 10
褲	糟	灣
see page 107	*see page 119*	*see page 123*
kù	zāo	wān

Lesson 11	Lesson 11	
鐵	讓	
see page 127	*see page 131*	
tiě	ràng	

Integrated Chinese I, Part 1 — Character Index
Chronological by Lesson
(Lessons 1-11, including Radicals and Numerals)

*	=	bound form
M	=	Measure word
P	=	Particle
QP	=	Question Particle

Radicals

人／亻	rén	man; person
刀／刂	dāo	knife
力	lì	power
又	yòu	right hand; again
口	kǒu	mouth
口	wéi	enclose
土	tǔ	earth
夕	xī	sunset
大	dà	big; large
女	nǚ	female; woman
子	zǐ	son; child
寸	cùn	inch
小	xiǎo	little; small
工	gōng	labor; work; craft
幺	yāo	tiny; small
弓	gōng	bow
心／忄	xīn	heart
戈	gē	dagger-axe
手／扌	shǒu	hand
日	rì	sun
月	yuè	moon
木	mù	wood
水／氵	shuǐ	water
火／灬	huǒ	fire
田	tián	field
目	mù	eye

示／礻	shì	to show
糸	mì	fine silk
耳	ěr	ear
衣／衤	yī	clothing
言	yán	word
貝	bèi	cowry shell
走	zǒu	to walk
足	zú	foot
金	jīn	metal; gold
門	mén	door; gate
隹	zhuī	short-tailed bird
雨	yǔ	rain
食	shí	to eat
馬	mǎ	horse

Numerals

一	yī	one
二	èr	two
三	sān	three
四	sì	four
五	wǔ	five
六	liù	six
七	qī	seven
八	bā	eight
九	jiǔ	nine
十	shí	ten

Lesson 1

先	xiān	first
生	shēng	born
你	nǐ	you
好	hǎo	good; fine; O.K.
小	xiǎo	little; small
姐	jiě	older sister
王	wáng	(a surname); king
李	lǐ	(a surname); plum
請/请	qǐng	please; invite
問/问	wèn	ask
您	nín	you (polite)
貴/贵	guì	honorable
姓	xìng	surname
我	wǒ	I; me
呢	ne	QP
叫	jiào	call
什(甚)	shén	*what
麼/么	me	*QP
名	míng	name
字	zì	character
朋	péng	friend
友	yǒu	friend
是	shì	be
老	lǎo	old
師/师	shī	teacher
嗎/吗	ma	QP
不	bù	not; no
學/学	xué	study
也	yě	also; too
中	zhōng	center; middle
國/国	guó	country
人	rén	man; person

美　měi　beautiful

Lesson 2

那	nà / nèi	that
張/张	zhāng	M
照	zhào	shine
片	piàn	*film; slice
的	de	P
這/这	zhè(i)	this
爸	bà	dad
媽/妈	mā	mom
個/个	gè	M (general)
男	nán	male
孩	hái	child
子	zǐ	son
誰/谁	shéi	who
他	tā	he
弟	dì	younger brother
女	nǔ	female
妹	mèi	younger sister
她	tā	she
兒/儿	ér	son; child
有	yǒu	have; there is/are
沒(没)	méi	(have) not
高	gāo	tall
家	jiā	family; home
幾/几	jǐ	QP; how many
哥	gē	older brother
兩/两	liǎng	two; a couple of
和	hé	and
做	zuò	do
英/英	yīng	*England
文	wén	script
律	lù	law; rule

都		dōu	all; both	白		bái	white

都		dōu	all; both
醫／医		yī	medicine; doctor

Lesson 3

月		yuè	moon; month
號／号		hào	number
星		xīng	star
期		qī	period (of time)
天		tiān	sky; day
日		rì	day
今		jīn	today; now
年		nián	year
多		duō	many
大		dà	big
歲／岁		suì	age
吃		chī	eat
晚		wǎn	evening; late
飯／饭		fàn	meal
怎		zěn	*how
樣／样		yàng	kind
太		tài	too; extremely
了		le	P
謝／谢		xiè	thank
喜		xǐ	*like; happy
歡／欢		huān	joyful
還／还		hái	still; yet
可		kě	but
們／们		men	*(plural suffix)
點／点		diǎn	dot; o'clock
鐘／钟		zhōng	clock
半		bàn	half
上		shàng	above; top
見／见		jiàn	see
再		zài	again

白		bái	white
現／现		xiàn	now
在		zài	at; in; on
刻		kè	quarter (hour)
明		míng	bright
忙		máng	busy
很		hěn	very
事		shì	affair; matter
為／为		wèi	for
因		yīn	because
同		tóng	same
認／认		rèn	recognize
識／识		shí	recognize

Lesson 4

週／周		zhōu	week
末		mò	end
打		dǎ	hit; strike
球		qiú	ball
看		kàn	see; look
電／电		diàn	electric
視／视		shì	view
唱		chàng	sing
歌		gē	song
跳		tiào	jump
舞		wǔ	dance
聽／听		tīng	listen
音		yīn	sound; music
樂／乐		yuè	music
對／对		duì	correct; toward
時／时		shí	time
候		hòu	wait
書／书		shū	book
影		yǐng	shadow

常	cháng	often		作	zuò	work; do
去	qù	go		校	xiào	school
外	wài	outside		喝	hē	drink
客	kè	guest		茶／茶	chá	tea
昨	zuó	yesterday		咖	kā	*coffee
所(所)	suǒ	*so; place		啡	fēi	*coffee
以	yǐ	with		啤	pí	*beer
久	jiǔ	long time		酒	jiǔ	wine
錯／错	cuò	wrong; error		吧	ba	P
想	xiǎng	think		要	yào	want
覺／觉	jué	feel; reckon		杯	bēi	cup; glass
得	dé	obtain; get		起	qǐ	rise
意	yì	meaning		給／给	gěi	give
思	sī	think		水	shuǐ	water
只	zhǐ	only		玩	wán	play; visit
睡	shuì	sleep		圖／图	tú	drawing
算	suàn	calculate; figure		館／馆	guǎn	accomodations
找	zhǎo	look for; seek		瓶	píng	bottle
別／别	bié	other		聊	liáo	chat
				才	cái	not until; only
				回	huí	return

Lesson 5

呀	ya	P
進／进	jìn	enter
快	kuài	fast; quick
來／来	lái	come
介	jiè	between
紹／绍	shào	carry on
下	xià	below; under
興／兴	xìng	mood; interest
漂	piào	*pretty
亮／亮	liàng	bright
坐	zuò	sit
哪	nǎ / něi	which
工	gōng	labor; work; craft

Lesson 6

話／话	huà	speech
喂	wèi	Hello!; Hey!
就	jiù	just
位	wèi	M (polite)
午	wǔ	noon
間／间	jiān	M (for rooms)
題／题	tí	topic; question
開／开	kāi	open
會／会	huì	meet
節／节	jié	M (for classes)
課／课	kè	class; lesson

級／级	jí	grade; level
考	kǎo	test
試／试	shì	try
後／后	hòu	after
空	kòng	free time
方	fāng	square; side
便	biàn	convenient
到	dào	go to; arrive
辦／办	bàn	manage
公	gōng	public
室	shì	room
行	xíng	all right; O.K.
等	děng	wait
氣／气	qì	air
幫／帮	bāng	help
練／练	liàn	drill
習／习	xí	practice
說／说	shuō	speak
啊	a	P
但	dàn	but
知	zhī	know
道	dào	road; way

Lesson 7

跟	gēn	with; and
助	zhù	assist
復／复	fù	duplicate
寫／写	xiě	write
慢	màn	slow
教／教	jiāo	teach
筆／笔	bǐ	pen
難／难	nán	difficult; hard
裡／里	lǐ	inside
第	dì	(ordinal prefix)

預／预	yù	prepare
語／语	yǔ	language
法	fǎ	method; way
容	róng	hold; contain; allow
易	yì	easy
懂／懂	dǒng	understand
詞／词	cí	word
漢／汉	hàn	Chinese
平	píng	level; even
早	zǎo	early
夜	yè	night
功	gōng	skill
真(眞)	zhēn	true; real
始	shǐ	begin
唸／念	niàn	read
錄／录	lù	record
帥／帅	shuài	handsome; smart

Lesson 8

篇	piān	M (for articles)
記／记	jì	record
床(牀)	chuáng	bed
洗	xǐ	wash
澡	zǎo	bath
邊／边	biān	side
發／发	fā	emit; issue
腦／脑	nǎo	brain
餐	cān	meal
廳／厅	tīng	hall
報／报	bào	newspaper
宿	sù	stay
舍	shè	house
正	zhèng	just; straight
前	qián	front; before

告	gào	tell; inform
訴／诉	sù	tell; relate
已	yǐ	already
經／经	jīng	pass through
封	fēng	M (for letters)
信	xìn	letter
最	zuì	most
近	jìn	near
除	chú	except
專／专	zhuān	special
業／业	yè	occupation
慣／惯	guàn	be used to
清	qíng	clear; clean
楚	chǔ	clear; neat
步	bù	step
希	xī	hope
望／望	wàng	hope; wish
能	néng	be able
用	yòng	use
笑	xiào	laugh
祝	zhù	wish

Lesson 9

買／买	mǎi	buy
東／东	dōng	east
西	xī	west
售	shòu	sell
貨／货	huò	merchandise
員／员	yuán	personnel
衣	yī	clothing
服	fú	clothing
件	jiàn	M (for items)
襯／衬	chèn	lining
衫	shān	shirt

顏／颜	yán	face; countenance
色	sè	color
黄(黄)	huáng	yellow
紅／红	hóng	red
穿	chuān	wear
條／条	tiáo	M (for long objects)
褲／裤	kù	pants
宜	yí	suitable
付	fù	pay
錢／钱	qián	money
共	gòng	altogether
少	shǎo	few
塊／块	kuài	piece; dollar
毛	máo	hair; dime
分	fēn	penny; minute
百	bǎi	hundred
雙／双	shuāng	pair
鞋	xié	shoes
換／换	huàn	change
黑	hēi	black
雖／虽	suī	though; while
然	rán	like that; so
合	hé	suit; agree
適／适	shì	suit; fit

Lesson 10

比	bǐ	compare
雨	yǔ	rain
更	gèng	even more
而	ér	and; in addition
且	qiě	for the time being
暖	nuǎn	warm
約／约	yuē	make an appoint.
園／园	yuán	garden

葉／叶	yè	leaf	
像	xiàng	image	
海	hǎi	sea	
糟	zāo	messy	
糕	gāo	cake	
又	yòu	again	
剛／刚	gāng	just now	
出	chū	go out	
熱／热	rè	hot	
舒	shū	stretch	
夏	xià	summer	
涼／凉	liáng	cool	
春	chūn	spring	
冬	dōng	winter	
冷	lěng	cold	
悶／闷	mēn	stuffy	
次	cì	M (for occurance)	
秋	qiū	autumn; fall	
台(臺)	tái	platform	
北	běi	north	
灣／湾	wān	strait; bay	

鐵／铁	tiě	iron	
走	zǒu	walk	
站	zhàn	stand; station	
綠／绿	lù	green	
線／线	xiàn	line	
藍／蓝	lán	blue	
麻	má	hemp; numb	
煩／烦	fán	bother	
租	zū	rent	
送	sòng	deliver	
過／过	guò	pass	
讓／让	ràng	let	
花／花	huā	spend	
每	měi	every	
速	sù	speed	
路	lù	road; way	
緊／紧	jǐn	tight	
自	zì	self	
己	jǐ	oneself	
新	xīn	new	
禮／礼	lǐ	gift	
物	wù	thing; matter	

Lesson 11

寒	hán	cold	
假	jià	vacation	
飛／飞	fēi	fly	
機／机	jī	machine	
票	piào	ticket	
場／场	chǎng	field	
汽	qì	steam	
車／车	chē	car	
或	huò	or	
者	zhě	(a suffix)	
地	dì	earth	

Integrated Chinese I, Part 1 — Character Index
Alphabetical by Pīnyīn

*	=	bound form
M	=	Measure word
P	=	Particle
QP	=	Question Particle

A

啊	a	P	6.2

B

八	bā	eight	Num
爸	bà	dad	2.1
吧	ba	P	5.1
白	bái	white	3.1
百	bǎi	hundred	9.1
半	bàn	half	3.1
辦／办	bàn	manage	6.1
幫／帮	bāng	help	6.2
報／报	bào	newspaper	8.1
杯	bēi	cup; glass	5.1
北	běi	north	10.2
貝／贝	bèi	cowry shell	Rad
筆／笔	bǐ	pen	7.1
比	bǐ	compare	10.1
邊／边	biān	side	8.1
便	biàn	convenient	6.1
別／别	bié	other	4.2
不	bù	not; no	1.3
步	bù	step	8.2

C

才	cái	not until; only	5.2
餐	cān	meal	8.1
茶／茶	chá	tea	5.1
常	cháng	often	4.1
場／场	chǎng	field	11.1
唱	chàng	sing	4.1
車／车	chē	car	11.1
襯／衬	chèn	lining	9.1
吃	chī	eat	3.1
出	chū	go out	10.2
除	chú	except	8.2
楚	chǔ	clear; neat	8.2
穿	chuān	wear	9.1
床(牀)	chuáng	bed	8.1
春	chūn	spring	10.2
詞／词	cí	word	7.1
次	cì	M (for occurances)	10.2
寸	cùn	inch	Rad
錯／错	cuò	wrong; error	4.2

D

打	dǎ	hit; strike	4.1
大	dà	big	Rad, 3.1
但	dàn	but	6.2
刀／刂	dāo	knife	Rad
到	dào	arrive	6.1
道	dào	road; way	6.2
得	dé	obtain; get	4.2
的	de	P	2.1
得	děi	must; have to	6.1 (4.2)
等	děng	wait	6.1

弟		dì	younger brother	2.1	高		gāo	tall	2.1

弟　　　dì　younger brother　2.1
第　　　dì　(ordinal prefix)　7.1
地　　　dì　earth　11.1
點／点　diǎn　dot; o'clock　3.1
電／电　diàn　electric　4.1
東／东　dōng　east　9.1
冬　　　dōng　winter　10.2
懂／懂　dǒng　understand　7.1
都　　　dōu　all; both　2.2
對／对　duì　correct; toward　4.1
多　　　duō　many　3.1

E

兒／儿　ér　son; child　2.1
而　　　ér　and　10.1
耳　　　ěr　ear　Rad
二　　　èr　two　Num

F

發／发　fā　emit; issue　8.1
法　　　fǎ　method; way　7.1
煩／烦　fán　bother　11.1
飯／饭　fàn　meal　3.1
方　　　fāng　square; side　6.1
啡　　　fēi　*coffee　5.1
飛／飞　fēi　fly　11.1
分　　　fēn　penny; minute　9.1
封　　　fēng　M (for letters)　8.2
服　　　fú　clothing　9.1
復／复　fù　duplicate　7.1
付　　　fù　pay　9.1

G

剛／刚　gāng　just now　10.2

高　　　gāo　tall　2.1
糕　　　gāo　cake　10.2
告　　　gào　tell; inform　8.1
戈　　　gē　dagger-axe　Rad
哥　　　gē　older brother　2.2
歌　　　gē　song　4.1
個／个　gè　M (general)　2.1
給／给　gěi　give　5.1
跟　　　gēn　with; and　7.1
更　　　gèng　even more　10.1
弓　　　gōng　bow　Rad
工　　　gōng　craft; work　Rad, 5.1
公　　　gōng　public　6.1
功　　　gōng　skill　7.2
共　　　gòng　altogether　9.1
館／馆　guǎn　accommodations　5.2
慣／惯　guàn　be used to　8.2
貴／贵　guì　honorable　1.2
國／国　guó　country　1.3
過／过　guò　pass　11.2

H

孩　　　hái　child　2.1
還／还　hái　still; yet　3.1
海　　　hǎi　sea　10.1
寒　　　hán　cold　11.1
漢／汉　hàn　Chinese　7.1
好　　　hǎo　fine; good; OK　1.1
號／号　hào　number　3.1
喝　　　hē　drink　5.1
和　　　hé　and　2.2
合　　　hé　suit; agree　9.2
黑　　　hēi　black　9.2
很　　　hěn　very　3.2

練／练	liàn	drill	6.2
涼／凉	liáng	cool	10.2
兩／两	liǎng	two; a couple	2.2
亮／亮	liàng	bright	5.1
聊	liáo	chat	5.2
六	liù	six	Num
錄／录	lù	record	7.2
路	lù	road; way	11.2
律	lǜ	law; rule	2.2
綠／绿	lǜ	green	11.1

M

媽／妈	mā	mom	2.1
麻	má	hemp; numb	11.1
馬／马	mǎ	horse	Rad
嗎／吗	ma	QP	1.3
買／买	mǎi	buy	9.1
慢	màn	slow	7.1
忙	máng	busy	3.2
毛	máo	hair; dime	9.1
麼／么	me	*QP	1.2
沒(没)	méi	(have) not	2.1
美	měi	beautiful	1.3
每	měi	every; each	11.2
妹	mèi	younger sister	2.1
悶／闷	mēn	stuffy	10.2
門／门	mén	door; gate	Rad
們／们	men	*(plural suffix)	3.1
糸	mì	fine silk	Rad
名	míng	name	1.2
明	míng	bright	3.2
末	mò	end	4.1
木	mù	wood	Rad
目	mù	eye	Rad

N

哪	nǎ / něi	which	5.1
那	nà / nèi	that	2.1
男	nán	male	2.1
難／难	nán	difficult; hard	7.1
腦／脑	nǎo	brain	8.1
呢	ne	QP	1.2
能	néng	be able	8.2
你	nǐ	you	1.1
年	nián	year	3.1
唸／念	niàn	read	7.2
您	nín	you (polite)	1.2
暖	nuǎn	warm	10.1
女	nǚ	woman; female	Rad, 2.1

P

朋	péng	friend	1.2
啤	pí	*beer	5.1
篇	piān	M (for articles)	8.1
便	pián	*inexpensive	9.1
片	piàn	slice; *film	2.1
漂	piào	*pretty	5.1
票	piào	ticket	11.1
瓶	píng	bottle	5.2
平	píng	level; even	7.2

Q

七	qī	seven	Num
期	qī	period (of time)	3.1
起	qǐ	rise	5.1
氣／气	qì	air	6.1
汽	qì	steam	11.1
前	qián	front; before	8.1

錢／钱	qián	money	9.1
且	qiě	for the time being	10.1
清	qīng	clear; clean	8.2
請／请	qǐng	please; invite	1.2
秋	qiū	autumn; fall	10.2
球	qiú	ball	4.1
去	qù	go	4.1

R

然	rán	like that; so	9.2
讓／让	ràng	let; allow	11.2
熱／热	rè	hot	10.2
人／亻	rén	man; person	Rad, 1.3
認／认	rèn	to recognize	3.2
日	rì	sun; day	Rad, 3.1
容	róng	hold; contain	7.1

S

三	sān	three	Num
色	sè	color	9.1
衫	shān	shirt	9.1
上	shàng	above; on top	3.1
少	shǎo	few	9.1
紹／绍	shào	carry on	5.1
舍	shè	house	8.1
誰／谁	shéi	who	2.1
什(甚)	shén	*what	1.2
生	shēng	be born	1.1
師／师	shī	teacher	1.3
食	shí	to eat	Rad
十	shí	ten	Num
識／识	shí	to recognize	3.2
時／时	shí	time	4.1
始	shǐ	begin	7.2

示／礻	shì	to show	Rad
是	shì	be	1.3
事	shì	matter; affair	3.2
視／视	shì	view	4.1
室	shì	room	6.1
試／试	shì	try	6.1
適／适	shì	suit; fit	9.2
手	shǒu	hand	Rad
售	shòu	sell	9.1
書／书	shū	book	4.1
舒	shū	stretch	10.2
帥／帅	shuài	handsome	7.2
雙／双	shuāng	pair	9.2
水／氵	shuǐ	water	Rad, 5.1
睡	shuì	sleep	4.2
說／说	shuō	speak	6.2
思	sī	think	4.2
四	sì	four	Num
送	sòng	deliver	11.1
宿	sù	stay	8.1
訴／诉	sù	tell; relate	8.1
速	sù	speed	11.2
算	suàn	stay	4.2
雖／虽	suī	though; while	9.2
歲／岁	suì	age	3.1
所(所)	suǒ	*so; place	4.1

T

他	tā	he	2.1
她	tā	she	2.1
台(臺)	tái	platform	10.2
太	tài	too; extremely	3.1
題／题	tí	topic; question	6.1
天	tiān	sky; day	3.1

田	tián	(a surname); field	Rad
條／条	tiáo	M (for long objects)	9.1
跳	tiào	jump	4.1
鐵／铁	tiě	iron	11.1
聽／听	tīng	listen	4.1
廳／厅	tīng	hall	8.1
同	tóng	same	3.2
圖／图	tú	drawing	5.2
土	tǔ	earth	Rad

W

外	wài	outside	4.1
灣／湾	wān	strait; bay	10.2
玩	wán	play; visit	5.2
晚	wǎn	evening; late	3.1
王	wáng	(a surname); king	1.1
望／望	wàng	hope; wish	8.2
囗	wéi	enclose	Rad
為／为	wèi	for	3.2
位	wèi	M (polite)	6.1
喂	wèi	Hello!; Hey!	6.1
文	wén	script	2.2
問／问	wèn	ask	1.2
我	wǒ	I; me	1.2
五	wǔ	five	Num
舞	wǔ	dance	4.1
午	wǔ	noon	6.1
物	wù	thing; matter	11.2

X

夕	xī	sunset	Rad
希	xī	hope	8.2
西	xī	west	9.1
習／习	xí	practice	6.2

喜	xǐ	like; happy	3.1
洗	xǐ	wash	8.1
下	xià	below; under	5.1
夏	xià	summer	10.2
先	xiān	first	1.1
現／现	xiàn	present	3.2
線／线	xiàn	line	11.1
想	xiǎng	think	4.2
像	xiàng	image	10.1
小	xiǎo	little; small	Rad, 1.1
校	xiào	school	5.1
笑	xiào	laugh	8.2
鞋	xié	shoes	9.2
寫／写	xiě	write	7.1
謝／谢	xiè	thank	3.1
心／忄	xīn	heart	Rad
新	xīn	new	11.2
信	xìn	letter	8.2
星	xīng	star	3.1
行	xíng	all right; O.K.	6.1
姓	xìng	surname	1.2
興／兴	xìng	mood; interest	5.1
學／学	xué	study	1.3

Y

呀	ya	P	5.1
言	yán	word	Rad
顏／颜	yán	face; countenance	9.1
樣／样	yàng	kind	3.1
幺	yāo	tiny; small	Rad
要	yào	want	5.1
也	yě	also	1.3
夜	yè	night	7.2
業／业	yè	occupation	8.2

葉／叶	yè	leaf	10.1
一	yī	one	Num
醫／医	yī	doctor; medicine	2.2
衣／衤	yī	clothing	Rad, 9.1
宜	yí	suitable	9.1
以	yǐ	with	4.1
已	yǐ	already	8.1
意	yì	meaning	4.2
易	yì	easy	7.1
因	yīn	because	3.2
音	yīn	sound; music	4.1
英／英	yīng	*England	2.2
影	yǐng	shadow	4.1
用	yòng	use	8.2
友	yǒu	friend	1.2
有	yǒu	have; there is/are	2.1
又	yòu	again	Rad, 10.2
語／语	yǔ	language	7.1
雨	yǔ	rain	Rad, 10.1
預／预	yù	prepare	7.1
員／员	yuán	personnel	9.1
園／园	yuán	garden	10.1
約／约	yuē	make an appoint.	10.1
月	yuè	moon; month	Rad, 3.1
樂／乐	yuè	music	4.1

Z

再	zài	again	3.1
在	zài	at; in; on	3.2
糟	zāo	messy	10.2
早	zǎo	early	7.2
澡	zǎo	bath	8.1
怎	zěn	*how	3.1
站	zhàn	stand; station	11.1
張／张	zhāng	M; (a surname)	2.1
找	zhǎo	look for; seek	4.2
照	zhào	shine	2.1
者	zhě	(a suffix)	11.1
這／这	zhè(i)	this	2.1
真(眞)	zhēn	true; real	7.2
正	zhèng	just; straight	8.1
知	zhī	know	6.2
只	zhǐ	only	4.2
中	zhōng	center; middle	1.3
鐘／钟	zhōng	clock	3.1
週／周	zhōu	week	4.1
助	zhù	assist	7.1
祝	zhù	wish	8.2
專／专	zhuān	special	8.2
隹	zhuī	short-tailed bird	Rad
子	zǐ	son	Rad, 2.1
字	zì	character	1.2
自	zì	self	11.2
走	zǒu	walk	Rad, 11.1
租	zū	rent	11.1
足	zú	foot	Rad
最	zuì	most	8.2
昨	zuó	yesterday	4.1
做	zuò	do	2.2
坐	zuò	sit	5.1
作	zuò	work; do	5.1

Integrated Chinese I, Part 1 — Character Index
Arranged by Number of Strokes

```
*    =    bound form
M    =    Measure word
P    =    Particle
QP   =    Question Particle
```

1

一   yī   one   Num

2

八   bā   eight   Num
刀／刂   dāo   knife   Rad
二   èr   two   Num
九   jiǔ   nine   Num
了   le   P   3.1
力   lì   power; strength   Rad
七   qī   seven   Num
人／亻   rén   man; person   Rad, 1.2
十   shí   ten   Num
又   yòu   again   Rad, 10.2

3

才   cái   not until; only   5.2
寸   cùn   inch   Rad
大   dà   big   Rad, 3.1
工   gōng   craft; work   Rad, 5.1
弓   gōng   bow   Rad
女   nǚ   woman; female   Rad, 2.1
己   jǐ   oneself   11.2
久   jiǔ   long time   4.2
口   kǒu   mouth   Rad
三   sān   three   Num
上   shàng   above; on top   3.1
土   tǔ   earth   Rad

口   wéi   enclose   Rad
夕   xī   sunset   Rad
下   xià   below; under   5.1
小   xiǎo   little; small   Rad, 1.1
幺   yāo   tiny; small   Rad
也   yě   also   1.2
已   yǐ   already   8.1
子   zǐ   son   Rad, 2.1

4

比   bǐ   compare   10.1
不   bù   not; no   1.2
方   fāng   square; side   6.1
分   fēn   penny; minute   9.1
戈   gē   dagger-axe   Rad
公   gōng   public   6.1
火／灬   huǒ   fire   Rad
介   jiè   between   5.1
今   jīn   today; now   3.1
六   liù   six   Num
毛   máo   hair; dime   9.1
木   mù   wood   Rad
片   piàn   slice; *film   2.1
日   rì   sun; day   Rad, 3.1
少   shǎo   few   9.1
什(甚)   shén   *what   1.1
手   shǒu   hand   Rad
水／氵   shuǐ   water   Rad, 5.1

太	tài	too; extremely	3.1
天	tiān	sky; day	3.1
王	wáng	(a surname); king	1.1
文	wén	script	2.2
五	wǔ	five	Num
午	wǔ	noon	6.1
心/忄	xīn	heart	Rad
以	yǐ	with	4.1
友	yǒu	friend	1.1
月	yuè	moon; month	Rad, 3.1
中	zhōng	center; middle	1.2

5

白	bái	white	3.1
半	bàn	half	3.1
北	běi	north	10.2
出	chū	go out	10.2
打	dǎ	hit; strike	4.1
冬	dōng	winter	10.2
付	fù	pay	9.1
功	gōng	skill	7.2
叫	jiào	call	1.1
可	kě	but	3.1
末	mò	end	4.1
目	mù	eye	Rad
平	píng	level; even	7.2
且	qiě	for the time being	10.1
去	qù	go	4.1
生	shēng	be born	1.1
示/礻	shì	to show	Rad
四	sì	four	Num
他	tā	he	2.1
台(臺)	tái	platform	10.2
田	tián	(a surname); field	Rad

外	wài	outside	4.1
用	yòng	use	8.2
正	zhèng	just; straight	8.1
只	zhǐ	only	4.2

6

百	bǎi	hundred	9.1
吃	chī	eat	3.1
次	cì	M (for occurances)	10.2
地	dì	earth	11.1
多	duō	many	3.1
而	ér	and	10.1
耳	ěr	ear	Rad
共	gòng	altogether	9.1
好	hǎo	fine; good; OK	1.1
合	hé	suit; agree	9.2
回	huí	return	5.2
件	jiàn	M (for items)	9.1
考	kǎo	test	6.1
老	lǎo	old	1.2
忙	máng	busy	3.2
糸	mì	fine silk	Rad
名	míng	name	1.1
年	nián	year	3.1
色	sè	color	9.1
她	tā	she	2.1
同	tóng	same	3.2
西	xī	west	9.1
先	xiān	first	1.1
行	xíng	all right; O.K.	6.1
衣/礻	yī	clothing	Rad, 9.1
因	yīn	because	3.2
有	yǒu	have; there is/are	2.1
再	zài	again	3.1

在	zài	at; in; on	3.2
早	zǎo	early	7.2
字	zì	character	1.1
自	zì	self	11.2

7

吧	ba	P	5.1
貝／贝	bèi	cowry shell	Rad
別／别	bié	other	4.2
步	bù	step	8.2
車／车	chē	car	11.1
床(牀)	chuáng	bed	8.1
但	dàn	but	6.2
弟	dì	younger brother	2.1
告	gào	tell; inform	8.1
更	gèng	even more	10.1
見／见	jiàn	see	3.1
快	kuài	fast; quick	5.1
冷	lěng	cold	10.2
李	lǐ	(a surname); plum	1.1
沒(沒)	méi	(have) not	2.1
每	měi	every; each	11.2
那	nà / nèi	that	2.1
男	nán	male	2.1
你	nǐ	you	1.1
汽	qì	steam	11.1
位	wèi	M (polite)	6.1
我	wǒ	I; me	1.1
希	xī	hope	8.2
言	yán	word	Rad
找	zhǎo	look for; seek	4.2
助	zhù	assist	7.1
走	zǒu	walk	Rad, 11.1
足	zú	foot	Rad

| 坐 | zuò | sit | 5.1 |
| 作 | zuò | work; do | 5.1 |

8

爸	bà	dad	2.1
杯	bēi	cup; glass	5.1
到	dào	arrive	6.1
的	de	P	2.1
東／东	dōng	east	9.1
兒／儿	ér	son; child	2.1
法	fǎ	method; way	7.1
服	fú	clothing	9.1
和	hé	and	2.2
花／花	huā	spend	11.2
或	huò	or	11.1
金	jīn	(a surname); gold	Rad
門／门	mén	door; gate	Rad
衫	shān	shirt	9.1
始	shǐ	begin	7.2
事	shì	matter; affair	3.2
所(所)	suǒ	*so; place	4.1
物	wù	thing; matter	11.2
姓	xìng	surname	1.1
夜	yè	night	7.2
宜	yí	suitable	9.1
易	yì	easy	7.1
雨	yǔ	rain	Rad, 10.1
隹	zhuī	short-tailed bird	Rad

9

便	biàn	convenient	6.1
穿	chuān	wear	9.1
春	chūn	spring	10.2
飛／飞	fēi	fly	11.1

封	fēng	M (for letters)	8.2
孩	hái	child	2.1
很	hěn	very	3.2
紅／红	hóng	red	9.1
後／后	hòu	after	6.1
看	kàn	see; look	4.1
客	kè	guest	4.1
亮／亮	liàng	bright	5.1
律	lù	law; rule	2.2
美	měi	beautiful	1.2
便	pián	*inexpensive	9.1
前	qián	front; before	8.1
秋	qiū	autumn; fall	10.2
食	shí	to eat	Rad
是	shì	be	1.2
室	shì	room	6.1
帥	shuài	handsome	7.2
思	sī	think	4.2
為／为	wèi	for	3.2
洗	xǐ	wash	8.1
信	xìn	letter	8.2
星	xīng	star	3.1
要	yào	want	5.1
音	yīn	sound; music	4.1
英／英	yīng	*England	2.2
約／约	yuē	make an appoint.	10.1
怎	zěn	*how	3.1
祝	zhù	wish	8.2
昨	zuó	yesterday	4.1

10

茶／茶	chá	tea	5.1
除	chú	except	8.2
剛／刚	gāng	just now	10.2

高	gāo	tall	2.1
哥	gē	older brother	2.2
個／个	gè	M (general)	2.1
海	hǎi	sea	10.1
級／级	jí	grade; level	6.1
記／记	jì	record	8.1
家	jiā	family; home	2.2
酒	jiǔ	wine	5.1
馬／马	mǎ	horse	Rad
們／们	men	*(plural suffix)	3.1
哪	nǎ / něi	which	5.1
能	néng	be able	8.2
瓶	píng	bottle	5.2
起	qǐ	rise	5.1
氣／气	qì	air	6.1
容	róng	hold; contain	7.1
師／师	shī	teacher	1.2
時／时	shí	time	4.1
書／书	shū	book	4.1
送	sòng	deliver	11.1
夏	xià	summer	10.2
校	xiào	school	5.1
笑	xiào	laugh	8.2
員／员	yuán	personnel	9.1
站	zhàn	stand; station	11.1
真(真)	zhēn	true; real	7.2
租	zū	rent	11.1

11

啊	a	P	6.2
常	cháng	often	4.1
唱	chàng	sing	4.1
得	dé	obtain; get	4.2
得	děi	must; have to	6.1 (4.2)

第	dì	(ordinal prefix)	7.1
都	dōu	all; both	2.2
啡	fēi	*coffee	5.1
國／国	guó	country	1.2
黃(黄)	huáng	yellow	9.1
貨／货	huò	merchandise	9.1
假	jià	vacation	11.1
教／教	jiāo	teach	7.1
涼／凉	liáng	cool	10.2
聊	liáo	chat	5.2
麻	má	hemp; numb	11.1
唸／念	niàn	read	7.2
您	nín	you (polite)	1.1
啤	pí	*beer	5.1
票	piào	ticket	11.1
清	qīng	clear; clean	8.2
球	qiú	ball	4.1
紹／绍	shào	carry on	5.1
視／视	shì	view	4.1
售	shòu	sell	9.1
宿	sù	stay	8.1
速	sù	speed	11.2
條／条	tiáo	M (for long objects)	9.1
望／望	wàng	hope; wish	8.2
問／问	wèn	ask	1.1
習／习	xí	practice	6.2
現／现	xiàn	present	3.2
張／张	zhāng	M; (a surname)	2.1
這／这	zhè(i)	this	2.1
專／专	zhuān	special	8.2
做	zuò	do	2.2

12

筆／笔	bǐ	pen	7.1
場／场	chǎng	field	11.1
詞／词	cí	word	7.1
等	děng	wait	6.1
發／发	fā	emit; issue	8.1
飯／饭	fàn	meal	3.1
復／复	fù	duplicate	7.1
給／给	gěi	give	5.1
貴／贵	guì	honorable	1.1
喝	hē	drink	5.1
黑	hēi	black	9.2
換／换	huàn	change	9.2
幾／几	jǐ	QP; how many	2.2
間／间	jiān	M (for rooms)	6.1
進／进	jìn	enter	5.1
就	jiù	just	6.1
開／开	kāi	open	6.1
裡／里	lǐ	inside	7.1
買／买	mǎi	buy	9.1
悶／闷	mēn	stuffy	10.2
期	qī	period (of time)	3.1
然	rán	like that; so	9.2
試／试	shì	try	6.1
舒	shu	stretch	10.2
訴／诉	sù	tell; relate	8.1
晚	wǎn	evening; late	3.1
喂	wèi	Hello!; Hey!	6.1
喜	xǐ	like; happy	3.1
葉／叶	yè	leaf	10.1
園／园	yuán	garden	10.1
週／周	zhōu	week	4.1
最	zuì	most	8.2

報／报	bào	newspaper	8.1

13

楚		chǔ	clear; neat	8.2
道		dào	road; way	6.2
電／电		diàn	electric	4.1
煩／烦		fán	bother	11.1
跟		gēn	with; and	6.2
過／过		guò	pass	11.2
號／号		hào	number	3.1
話／话		huà	speech	6.1
會／会		huì	meet	6.1
塊／块		kuài	piece; dollar	9.1
節／节		jié	M (for classes)	6.1
經／经		jīng	pass through	8.1
路		lù	road; way	11.2
媽／妈		mā	mom	2.1
嗎／吗		ma	QP	1.2
腦／脑		nǎo	brain	8.1
暖		nuǎn	warm	10.1
睡		shuì	sleep	4.2
歲／岁		suì	age	3.1
跳		tiào	jump	4.1
想		xiǎng	think	4.2
新		xīn	new	11.2
業／业		yè	occupation	8.2
意		yì	meaning	4.2
預／预		yù	prepare	7.1
照		zhào	shine	2.1

14

對／对		duì	correct; toward	4.1
歌		gē	song	4.1
慣／惯		guàn	be used to	8.2
漢／汉		hàn	Chinese	7.1

緊／紧		jǐn	tight	11.2
綠／绿		lù	green	11.1
慢		màn	slow	7.1
麼／么		me	*QP	1.1
漂		piào	*pretty	5.1
認／认		rèn	to recognize	3.2
說／说		shuō	speak	6.2
算		suàn	stay	4.2
圖／图		tú	drawing	5.2
舞		wǔ	dance	4.1
像		xiàng	image	10.1
寫／写		xiě	write	7.1
語／语		yǔ	language	7.1

15

課／课		kè	class; lesson	6.1
褲／裤		kù	pants	9.1
樂／乐		lè	happy	5.1 (4.1)
練／练		liàn	drill	6.2
篇		piān	M (for articles)	8.1
請／请		qǐng	please; invite	1.1
熱／热		rè	hot	10.2
誰／谁		shéi	who	2.1
適／适		shì	suit; fit	9.2
線／线		xiàn	line	11.1
鞋		xié	shoes	9.2
樣／样		yàng	kind	3.1
影		yǐng	shadow	4.1
樂／乐		yuè	music	4.1

16

辦／办		bàn	manage	6.1
餐		cān	meal	8.1
錯／错		cuò	wrong; error	4.2